Mary Stuart
A Tragedy

Frederich Schiller

Contents

DRAMATIS PERSONAE...7
ACT I. 8
ACT II..61
ACT III. 111
ACT IV. 143
ACT V...185

MARY STUART
A TRAGEDY

BY

Frederich Schiller

DRAMATIS PERSONAE.

ELIZABETH, Queen of England.
MARY STUART, Queen of Scots, a Prisoner in England.
ROBERT DUDLEY, Earl of Leicester.
GEORGE TALBOT, Earl of Shrewsbury.
WILLIAM CECIL, Lord Burleigh, Lord High Treasurer.
EARL OF KENT.
SIR WILLIAM DAVISON, Secretary of State.
SIR AMIAS PAULET, Keeper of MARY.
SIR EDWARD MORTIMER, his Nephew.
COUNT L'AUBESPINE, the French Ambassador.
O'KELLY, Mortimer's Friend.
COUNT BELLIEVRE, Envoy Extraordinary from France.
SIR DRUE DRURY, another Keeper of MARY.
SIR ANDREW MELVIL, her House Steward.
BURGOYNE, her Physician.
HANNAH KENNEDY, her Nurse.
MARGARET CURL, her Attendant.
Sheriff of the County.
Officer of the Guard.
French and English Lords.
Soldiers.
Servants of State belonging to ELIZABETH.
Servants and Female Attendants of the Queen of Scots.

ACT I.

SCENE I.

A common apartment in the Castle of Fotheringay.

HANNAH KENNEDY, contending violently with PAULET, who is about to break open a closet; DRURY with an iron crown.

KENNEDY.
How now, sir? what fresh outrage have we here?
Back from that cabinet!

PAULET.
      Whence came the jewel?
I know 'twas from an upper chamber thrown;
And you would bribe the gardener with your trinkets.
A curse on woman's wiles! In spite of all
My strict precaution and my active search,
Still treasures here, still costly gems concealed!
And doubtless there are more where this lay hid.

[Advancing towards the cabinet.

KENNEDY.
Intruder, back! here lie my lady's secrets.

PAULET.
Exactly what I seek.
    [Drawing forth papers.

KENNEDY.
    Mere trifling papers;
The amusements only of an idle pen,
To cheat the dreary tedium of a dungeon.

PAULET.
In idle hours the evil mind is busy.

KENNEDY.
Those writings are in French.

PAULET.
    So much the worse!
That tongue betokens England's enemy.

KENNEDY.
Sketches of letters to the Queen of England.

PAULET.
I'll be their bearer. Ha! what glitters here?

  [He touches a secret spring, and draws out jewels from
  a private drawer.

A royal diadem enriched with stones,
And studded with the fleur-de-lis of France.

  [He hands it to his assistant.

Here, take it, Drury; lay it with the rest.

[Exit DRURY.

[And ye have found the means to hide from us
Such costly things, and screen them, until now,
From our inquiring eyes?]

KENNEDY.
      Oh, insolent
And tyrant power, to which we must submit.

PAULET.
She can work ill as long as she hath treasures;
For all things turn to weapons in her hands.

KENNEDY (supplicating).
Oh, sir! be merciful; deprive us not
Of the last jewel that adorns our life!
'Tis my poor lady's only joy to view
This symbol of her former majesty;
Your hands long since have robbed us of the rest.

PAULET.
'Tis in safe custody; in proper time
'Twill be restored to you with scrupulous care.

KENNEDY.
Who that beholds these naked walls could say
That majesty dwelt here? Where is the throne?
Where the imperial canopy of state?
Must she not set her tender foot, still used
To softest treading, on the rugged ground?

With common pewter, which the lowliest dame
Would scorn, they furnish forth her homely table.

PAULET.
Thus did she treat her spouse at Stirling once;
And pledged, the while, her paramour in gold.

KENNEDY.
Even the mirror's trifling aid withheld.

PAULET.
The contemplation of her own vain image
Incites to hope, and prompts to daring deeds.

KENNEDY.
Books are denied her to divert her mind.

PAULET.
The Bible still is left to mend her heart.

KENNEDY.
Even of her very lute she is deprived!

PAULET.
Because she tuned it to her wanton airs.

KENNEDY.
Is this a fate for her, the gentle born,
Who in her very cradle was a queen?
Who, reared in Catherine's luxurious court,
Enjoyed the fulness of each earthly pleasure?
Was't not enough to rob her of her power,
Must ye then envy her its paltry tinsel?

A noble heart in time resigns itself
To great calamities with fortitude;
But yet it cuts one to the soul to part
At once with all life's little outward trappings!

PAULET.
These are the things that turn the human heart
To vanity, which should collect itself
In penitence; for a lewd, vicious life,
Want and abasement are the only penance.

KENNEDY.
If youthful blood has led her into error,
With her own heart and God she must account:
There is no judge in England over her.

PAULET.
She shall have judgment where she hath transgressed.

KENNEDY.
Her narrow bonds restrain her from transgression.

PAULET.
And yet she found the means to stretch her arm
Into the world, from out these narrow bonds,
And, with the torch of civil war, inflame
This realm against our queen (whom God preserve).
And arm assassin bands. Did she not rouse
From out these walls the malefactor Parry,
And Babington, to the detested crime
Of regicide? And did this iron grate
Prevent her from decoying to her toils
The virtuous heart of Norfolk? Saw we not

The first, best head in all this island fall
A sacrifice for her upon the block?
[The noble house of Howard fell with him.]
And did this sad example terrify
These mad adventurers, whose rival zeal
Plunges for her into this deep abyss?
The bloody scaffold bends beneath the weight
Of her new daily victims; and we ne'er
Shall see an end till she herself, of all
The guiltiest, be offered up upon it.
Oh! curses on the day when England took
This Helen to its hospitable arms.

KENNEDY.
Did England then receive her hospitably?
Oh, hapless queen! who, since that fatal day
When first she set her foot within this realm,
And, as a suppliant--a fugitive--
Came to implore protection from her sister,
Has been condemned, despite the law of nations,
And royal privilege, to weep away
The fairest years of youth in prison walls.
And now, when she hath suffered everything
Which in imprisonment is hard and bitter,
Is like a felon summoned to the bar,
Foully accused, and though herself a queen,
Constrained to plead for honor and for life.

PAULET.
She came amongst us as a murderess,
Chased by her very subjects from a throne
Which she had oft by vilest deeds disgraced.
Sworn against England's welfare came she hither,

To call the times of bloody Mary back,
Betray our church to Romish tyranny,
And sell our dear-bought liberties to France.
Say, why disdained she to subscribe the treaty
Of Edinborough--to resign her claim
To England's crown--and with one single word,
Traced by her pen, throw wide her prison gates?
No:--she had rather live in vile confinement,
And see herself ill-treated, than renounce
The empty honors of her barren title.
Why acts she thus? Because she trusts to wiles,
And treacherous arts of base conspiracy;
And, hourly plotting schemes of mischief, hopes
To conquer, from her prison, all this isle.

KENNEDY.
You mock us, sir, and edge your cruelty
With words of bitter scorn:--that she should form
Such projects; she, who's here immured alive,
To whom no sound of comfort, not a voice
Of friendship comes from her beloved home;
Who hath so long no human face beheld,
Save her stern gaoler's unrelenting brows;
Till now, of late, in your uncourteous cousin
She sees a second keeper, and beholds
Fresh bolts and bars against her multiplied.

PAULET.
No iron-grate is proof against her wiles.
How do I know these bars are not filed through?
How that this floor, these walls, that seem so strong
Without, may not be hollow from within,
And let in felon treachery when I sleep?

Accursed office, that's intrusted to me,
To guard this cunning mother of all ill!
Fear scares me from my sleep; and in the night
I, like a troubled spirit, roam and try
The strength of every bolt, and put to proof
Each guard's fidelity:--I see, with fear,
The dawning of each morn, which may confirm
My apprehensions:--yet, thank God, there's hope
That all my fears will soon be at an end;
For rather would I at the gates of hell
Stand sentinel, and guard the devilish host
Of damned souls, than this deceitful queen.

KENNEDY.
Here comes the queen.

PAULET.
    Christ's image in her hand.
Pride, and all worldly lusts within her heart.

SCENE II.

  The same. Enter MARY, veiled, a crucifix in her hand.

KENNEDY (hastening toward her).
O gracious queen! they tread us under foot;
No end of tyranny and base oppression;
Each coming day heaps fresh indignities,
New sufferings on thy royal head.

MARY.

          Be calm--
Say, what has happened?

KENNEDY.
          See! thy cabinet
Is forced--thy papers--and thy only treasure,
Which with such pains we had secured, the last
Poor remnant of thy bridal ornaments
From France, is in his hands--naught now remains
Of royal state--thou art indeed bereft!

MARY.
Compose yourself, my Hannah! and believe me,
'Tis not these baubles that can make a queen--
Basely indeed they may behave to us,
But they cannot debase us. I have learned
To use myself to many a change in England;
I can support this too. Sir, you have taken
By force what I this very day designed
To have delivered to you. There's a letter
Amongst these papers for my royal sister
Of England. Pledge me, sir, your word of honor,
To give it to her majesty's own hands,
And not to the deceitful care of Burleigh.

PAULET.
I shall consider what is best to do.

MARY.
Sir, you shall know its import. In this letter
I beg a favor, a great favor of her,--
That she herself will give me audience,--she
Whom I have never seen. I have been summoned

Before a court of men, whom I can ne'er
Acknowledge as my peers--of men to whom
My heart denies its confidence. The queen
Is of my family, my rank, my sex;
To her alone--a sister, queen, and woman--
Can I unfold my heart.

PAULET.
    Too oft, my lady,
Have you intrusted both your fate and honor
To men less worthy your esteem than these.

MARY.
I, in the letter, beg another favor,
And surely naught but inhumanity
Can here reject my prayer. These many years
Have I, in prison, missed the church's comfort,
The blessings of the sacraments--and she
Who robs me of my freedom and my crown,
Who seeks my very life, can never wish
To shut the gates of heaven upon my soul.

PAULET.
Whene'er you wish, the dean shall wait upon you.

MARY (interrupting him sharply).
Talk to me not of deans. I ask the aid
Of one of my own church--a Catholic priest.

PAULET.
[That is against the published laws of England.

MARY.

The laws of England are no rule for me.
I am not England's subject; I have ne'er
Consented to its laws, and will not bow
Before their cruel and despotic sway.
If 'tis your will, to the unheard-of rigor
Which I have borne, to add this new oppression,
I must submit to what your power ordains;
Yet will I raise my voice in loud complaints.]
I also wish a public notary,
And secretaries, to prepare my will--
My sorrows and my prison's wretchedness
Prey on my life--my days, I fear, are numbered--
I feel that I am near the gates of death.

PAULET.
These serious contemplations well become you.

MARY.
And know I then that some too ready hand
May not abridge this tedious work of sorrow?
I would indite my will and make disposal
Of what belongs tome.

PAULET.
            This liberty
May be allowed to you, for England's queen
Will not enrich herself by plundering you.

MARY.
I have been parted from my faithful women,
And from my servants; tell me, where are they?
What is their fate? I can indeed dispense
At present with their service, but my heart

Will feel rejoiced to know these faithful ones
Are not exposed to suffering and to want!

PAULET.
Your servants have been cared for; [and again
You shall behold whate'er is taken from you
And all shall be restored in proper season.]

    [Going.

MARY.
And will you leave my presence thus again,
And not relieve my fearful, anxious heart
From the fell torments of uncertainty?
Thanks to the vigilance of your hateful spies,
I am divided from the world; no voice
Can reach me through these prison-walls; my fate
Lies in the hands of those who wish my ruin.
A month of dread suspense is passed already
Since when the forty high commissioners
Surprised me in this castle, and erected,
With most unseemly haste, their dread tribunal;
They forced me, stunned, amazed, and unprepared,
Without an advocate, from memory,
Before their unexampled court, to answer
Their weighty charges, artfully arranged.
They came like ghosts,--like ghosts they disappeared,
And since that day all mouths are closed to me.
In vain I seek to construe from your looks
Which hath prevailed--my cause's innocence
And my friends' zeal--or my foes' cursed counsel.
Oh, break this silence! let me know the worst;
What have I still to fear, and what to hope.

PAULET.
Close your accounts with heaven.

MARY.
    From heaven I hope
For mercy, sir; and from my earthly judges
I hope, and still expect, the strictest justice.

PAULET.
Justice, depend upon it, will be done you.

MARY.
Is the suit ended, sir?

PAULET.
   I cannot tell.

MARY.
Am I condemned?

PAULET.
   I cannot answer, lady.

MARY.
[Sir, a good work fears not the light of day.

PAULET.
The day will shine upon it, doubt it not.]

MARY.
Despatch is here the fashion. Is it meant
The murderer shall surprise me, like the judges?

PAULET.
Still entertain that thought and he will find you
Better prepared to meet your fate than they did.

MARY (after a pause).
Sir, nothing can surprise me which a court
Inspired by Burleigh's hate and Hatton's zeal,
Howe'er unjust, may venture to pronounce:
But I have yet to learn how far the queen
Will dare in execution of the sentence.

PAULET.
The sovereigns of England have no fear
But for their conscience and their parliament.
What justice hath decreed her fearless hand
Will execute before the assembled world.

SCENE III.

> The same. MORTIMER enters, and without paying attention to the QUEEN, addresses PAULET.

MORTIMER.
Uncle, you're sought for.

> [He retires in the same manner. The QUEEN remarks it, and turns towards PAULET, who is about to follow him.

MARY.
    Sir, one favor more

If you have aught to say to me--from you
I can bear much--I reverence your gray hairs;
But cannot bear that young man's insolence;
Spare me in future his unmannered rudeness.

PAULET.
I prize him most for that which makes you hate him
He is not, truly, one of those poor fools
Who melt before a woman's treacherous tears.
He has seen much--has been to Rheims and Paris,
And brings us back his true old English heart.
Lady, your cunning arts are lost on him.

    [Exit.

SCENE IV.

  MARY, KENNEDY.

KENNEDY.
And dare the ruffian venture to your face
Such language! Oh, 'tis hard--'tis past endurance.

MARY (lost in reflection).
In the fair moments of our former splendor
We lent to flatterers a too willing ear;--
It is but just, good Hannah, we should now
Be forced to hear the bitter voice of censure.

KENNEDY.
So downcast, so depressed, my dearest lady!

You, who before so gay, so full of hope,
Were used to comfort me in my distress;
More gracious were the task to check your mirth
Than chide your heavy sadness.

MARY.
      Well I know him--
It is the bleeding Darnley's royal shade,
Rising in anger from his darksome grave
And never will he make his peace with me
Until the measures of my woes be full.

KENNEDY.
What thoughts are these--

MARY.
      Thou may'st forget it, Hannah;
But I've a faithful memory--'tis this day
Another wretched anniversary
Of that regretted, that unhappy deed--
Which I must celebrate with fast and penance.

KENNEDY.
Dismiss at length in peace this evil spirit.
The penitence of many a heavy year,
Of many a suffering, has atoned the deed;
The church, which holds the key of absolution,
Pardons the crime, and heaven itself's appeased.

MARY.
This long-atoned crime arises fresh
And bleeding from its lightly-covered grave;
My husband's restless spirit seeks revenge;

No sacred bell can exorcise, no host
In priestly hands dismiss it to his tomb.

KENNEDY.
You did not murder him; 'twas done by others.

MARY.
But it was known to me; I suffered it,
And lured him with my smiles to death's embrace.

KENNEDY.
Your youth extenuates your guilt. You were
Of tender years.

MARY.
    So tender, yet I drew
This heavy guilt upon my youthful head.

KENNEDY.
You were provoked by direst injuries,
And by the rude presumption of the man,
Whom out of darkness, like the hand of heaven,
Your love drew forth, and raised above all others.
Whom through your bridal chamber you conducted
Up to your throne, and with your lovely self,
And your hereditary crown, distinguished
[Your work was his existence, and your grace
Bedewed him like the gentle rains of heaven.]
Could he forget that his so splendid lot
Was the creation of your generous love?
Yet did he, worthless as he was, forget it.
With base suspicions, and with brutal manners,
He wearied your affections, and became

An object to you of deserved disgust:
The illusion, which till now had overcast
Your judgment, vanished; angrily you fled
His foul embrace, and gave him up to scorn.
And did he seek again to win your love?
Your favor? Did he e'er implore your pardon?
Or fall in deep repentance at your feet?
No; the base wretch defied you; he, who was
Your bounty's creature, wished to play your king,
[And strove, through fear, to force your inclination.]
Before your eyes he had your favorite singer,
Poor Rizzio, murdered; you did but avenge
With blood the bloody deed----

MARY.
      And bloodily,
I fear, too soon 'twill be avenged on me:
You seek to comfort me, and you condemn me.

KENNEDY.
You were, when you consented to this deed,
No more yourself; belonged not to yourself;
The madness of a frantic love possessed you,
And bound you to a terrible seducer,
The wretched Bothwell. That despotic man
Ruled you with shameful, overbearing will,
And with his philters and his hellish arts
Inflamed your passions.

MARY.
      All the arts he used
Were man's superior strength and woman's weakness.

KENNEDY.
No, no, I say. The most pernicious spirits
Of hell he must have summoned to his aid,
To cast this mist before your waking senses.
Your ear no more was open to the voice
Of friendly warning, and your eyes were shut
To decency; soft female bashfulness
Deserted you; those cheeks, which were before
The seat of virtuous, blushing modesty,
Glowed with the flames of unrestrained desire.
You cast away the veil of secrecy,
And the flagitious daring of the man
O'ercame your natural coyness: you exposed
Your shame, unblushingly, to public gaze:
You let the murderer, whom the people followed
With curses, through the streets of Edinburgh,
Before you bear the royal sword of Scotland
In triumph. You begirt your parliament
With armed bands; and by this shameless farce,
There, in the very temple of great justice,
You forced the judges of the land to clear
The murderer of his guilt. You went still further--
O God!

MARY.
   Conclude--nay, pause not--say for this
I gave my hand in marriage at the altar.

KENNEDY.
O let an everlasting silence veil
That dreadful deed: the heart revolts at it.
A crime to stain the darkest criminal!
Yet you are no such lost one, that I know.

I nursed your youth myself--your heart is framed
For tender softness: 'tis alive to shame,
And all your fault is thoughtless levity.
Yes, I repeat it, there are evil spirits,
Who sudden fix in man's unguarded breast
Their fatal residence, and there delight
To act their dev'lish deeds; then hurry back
Unto their native hell, and leave behind
Remorse and horror in the poisoned bosom.
Since this misdeed, which blackens thus your life,
You have done nothing ill; your conduct has
Been pure; myself can witness your amendment.
Take courage, then; with your own heart make peace.
Whatever cause you have for penitence,
You are not guilty here. Nor England's queen,
Nor England's parliament can be your judge.
Here might oppresses you: you may present
Yourself before this self-created court
With all the fortitude of innocence.

MARY.
I hear a step.

KENNEDY.
   It is the nephew--In.

SCENE V.

   The same. Enter MORTIMER, approaching cautiously.

MORTIMER (to KENNEDY).

Step to the door, and keep a careful watch,
I have important business with the queen.

MARY (with dignity).
I charge thee, Hannah, go not hence--remain.

MORTIMER.
Fear not, my gracious lady--learn to know me.

   [He gives her a card.

MARY (She examines it, and starts back astonished).
Heavens! What is this?

MORTIMER (to KENNEDY).
          Retire, good Kennedy;
See that my uncle comes not unawares.

MARY (to KENNEDY, who hesitates, and looks at the QUEEN inquiringly).
Go in; do as he bids you.

   [KENNEDY retires with signs of wonder.

SCENE VI.

   MARY, MORTIMER.

MARY.
          From my uncle
In France--the worthy Cardinal of Lorrain?

[She reads.

"Confide in Mortimer, who brings you this;
You have no truer, firmer friend in England."

[Looking at him with astonishment.

Can I believe it? Is there no delusion
To cheat my senses? Do I find a friend
So near, when I conceived myself abandoned
By the whole world? And find that friend in you,
The nephew of my gaoler, whom I thought
My most inveterate enemy?

MORTIMER (kneeling).
     Oh, pardon,
My gracious liege, for the detested mask,
Which it has cost me pain enough to wear;
Yet through such means alone have I the power
To see you, and to bring you help and rescue.

MARY.
Arise, sir; you astonish me; I cannot
So suddenly emerge from the abyss
Of wretchedness to hope: let me conceive
This happiness, that I may credit it.

MORTIMER.
Our time is brief: each moment I expect
My uncle, whom a hated man attends;
Hear, then, before his terrible commission
Surprises you, how heaven prepares your rescue.

MARY.
You come in token of its wondrous power.

MORTIMER.
Allow me of myself to speak.

MARY.
    Say on.

MORTIMER.
I scarce, my liege, had numbered twenty years,
Trained in the path of strictest discipline
And nursed in deadliest hate to papacy,
When led by irresistible desire
For foreign travel, I resolved to leave
My country and its puritanic faith
Far, far behind me: soon with rapid speed
I flew through France, and bent my eager course
On to the plains of far-famed Italy.
'Twas then the time of the great jubilee:
And crowds of palmers filled the public roads;
Each image was adorned with garlands; 'twas
As if all human-kind were wandering forth
In pilgrimage towards the heavenly kingdom.
The tide of the believing multitude
Bore me too onward, with resistless force,
Into the streets of Rome. What was my wonder,
As the magnificence of stately columns
Rushed on my sight! the vast triumphal arches,
The Colosseum's grandeur, with amazement
Struck my admiring senses; the sublime
Creative spirit held my soul a prisoner
In the fair world of wonders it had framed.

I ne'er had felt the power of art till now.
The church that reared me hates the charms of sense;
It tolerates no image, it adores
But the unseen, the incorporeal word.
What were my feelings, then, as I approached
The threshold of the churches, and within,
Heard heavenly music floating in the air:
While from the walls and high-wrought roofs there streamed
Crowds of celestial forms in endless train--
When the Most High, Most Glorious pervaded
My captivated sense in real presence!
And when I saw the great and godlike visions,
The Salutation, the Nativity,
The Holy Mother, and the Trinity's
Descent, the luminous transfiguration
And last the holy pontiff, clad in all
The glory of his office, bless the people!
Oh! what is all the pomp of gold and jewels
With which the kings of earth adorn themselves!
He is alone surrounded by the Godhead;
His mansion is in truth an heavenly kingdom,
For not of earthly moulding are these forms!

MARY.
O spare me, sir! No further. Spread no more
Life's verdant carpet out before my eyes,
Remember I am wretched, and a prisoner.

MORTIMER.
I was a prisoner, too, my queen; but swift
My prison-gates flew open, when at once
My spirit felt its liberty, and hailed
The smiling dawn of life. I learned to burst

Each narrow prejudice of education,
To crown my brow with never-fading wreaths,
And mix my joy with the rejoicing crowd.
Full many noble Scots, who saw my zeal,
Encouraged me, and with the gallant French
They kindly led me to your princely uncle,
The Cardinal of Guise. Oh, what a man!
How firm, how clear, how manly, and how great!
Born to control the human mind at will!
The very model of a royal priest;
A ruler of the church without an equal!

MARY.
You've seen him then,--the much loved, honored man,
Who was the guardian of my tender years!
Oh, speak of him! Does he remember me?
Does fortune favor him? And prospers still
His life? And does he still majestic stand,
A very rock and pillar of the church?

MORTIMER.
The holy man descended from his height,
And deigned to teach me the important creed
Of the true church, and dissipate my doubts.
He showed me how the glimmering light of reason
Serves but to lead us to eternal error:
That what the heart is called on to believe
The eye must see: that he who rules the church
Must needs be visible; and that the spirit
Of truth inspired the councils of the fathers.
How vanished then the fond imaginings
And weak conceptions of my childish soul
Before his conquering judgment, and the soft

Persuasion of his tongue! So I returned
Back to the bosom of the holy church,
And at his feet abjured my heresies.

MARY.
Then of those happy thousands you are one,
Whom he, with his celestial eloquence,
Like the immortal preacher of the mount,
Has turned and led to everlasting joy!

MORTIMER.
The duties of his office called him soon
To France, and I was sent by him to Rheims,
Where, by the Jesuits' anxious labor, priests
Are trained to preach our holy faith in England.
There, 'mongst the Scots, I found the noble Morgan,
And your true Lesley, Ross's learned bishop,
Who pass in France their joyless days of exile.
I joined with heartfelt zeal these worthy men,
And fortified my faith. As I one day
Roamed through the bishop's dwelling, I was struck
With a fair female portrait; it was full
Of touching wond'rous charms; with magic might
It moved my inmost soul, and there I stood
Speechless, and overmastered by my feelings.
"Well," cried the bishop, "may you linger thus
In deep emotion near this lovely face!
For the most beautiful of womankind,
Is also matchless in calamity.
She is a prisoner for our holy faith,
And in your native land, alas! she suffers."

[MARY is in great agitation. He pauses.

MARY.
Excellent man! All is not lost, indeed,
While such a friend remains in my misfortunes!

MORTIMER.
Then he began, with moving eloquence,
To paint the sufferings of your martyrdom;
He showed me then your lofty pedigree,
And your descent from Tudor's royal house.
He proved to me that you alone have right
To reign in England, not this upstart queen,
The base-born fruit of an adult'rous bed,
Whom Henry's self rejected as a bastard.
[He from my eyes removed delusion's mist,
And taught me to lament you as a victim,
To honor you as my true queen, whom I,
Deceived, like thousands of my noble fellows,
Had ever hated as my country's foe.]
I would not trust his evidence alone;
I questioned learned doctors; I consulted
The most authentic books of heraldry;
And every man of knowledge whom I asked
Confirmed to me your claim's validity.
And now I know that your undoubted right
To England's throne has been your only wrong,
This realm is justly yours by heritage,
In which you innocently pine as prisoner.

MARY.
Oh, this unhappy right!--'tis this alone
Which is the source of all my sufferings.

MORTIMER.
Just at this time the tidings reached my ears
Of your removal from old Talbot's charge,
And your committal to my uncle's care.
It seemed to me that this disposal marked
The wond'rous, outstretched hand of favoring heaven;
It seemed to be a loud decree of fate,
That it had chosen me to rescue you.
My friends concur with me; the cardinal
Bestows on me his counsel and his blessing,
And tutors me in the hard task of feigning.
The plan in haste digested, I commenced
My journey homewards, and ten days ago
On England's shores I landed. Oh, my queen.

[He pauses.

I saw then, not your picture, but yourself--
Oh, what a treasure do these walls enclose!
No prison this, but the abode of gods,
More splendid far than England's royal court.
Happy, thrice happy he, whose envied lot
Permits to breathe the selfsame air with you!
It is a prudent policy in her
To bury you so deep! All England's youth
Would rise at once in general mutiny,
And not a sword lie quiet in its sheath:
Rebellion would uprear its giant head,
Through all this peaceful isle, if Britons once
Beheld their captive queen.

MARY.
       'Twere well with her,

If every Briton saw her with your eyes!

MORTIMER.
Were each, like me, a witness of your wrongs,
Your meekness, and the noble fortitude
With which you suffer these indignities--
Would you not then emerge from all these trials
Like a true queen? Your prison's infamy,
Hath it despoiled your beauty of its charms?
You are deprived of all that graces life,
Yet round you life and light eternal beam.
Ne'er on this threshold can I set my foot,
That my poor heart with anguish is not torn,
Nor ravished with delight at gazing on you.
Yet fearfully the fatal time draws near,
And danger hourly growing presses on.
I can delay no longer--can no more
Conceal the dreadful news.

MARY.
      My sentence then!
It is pronounced? Speak freely--I can bear it.

MORTIMER.
It is pronounced! The two-and-forty judges
Have given the verdict, "guilty"; and the Houses
Of Lords and Commons, with the citizens
Of London, eagerly and urgently
Demand the execution of the sentence:--
The queen alone still craftily delays,
That she may be constrained to yield, but not
From feelings of humanity or mercy.

MARY (collected).
Sir, I am not surprised, nor terrified.
I have been long prepared for such a message.
Too well I know my judges. After all
Their cruel treatment I can well conceive
They dare not now restore my liberty.
I know their aim: they mean to keep me here
In everlasting bondage, and to bury,
In the sepulchral darkness of my prison,
My vengeance with me, and my rightful claims.

MORTIMER.
Oh, no, my gracious queen;--they stop not there:
Oppression will not be content to do
Its work by halves:--as long as e'en you live,
Distrust and fear will haunt the English queen.
No dungeon can inter you deep enough;
Your death alone can make her throne secure.

MARY.
Will she then dare, regardless of the shame,
Lay my crowned head upon the fatal block?

MORTIMER.
She will most surely dare it, doubt it not.

MARY.
And can she thus roll in the very dust
Her own, and every monarch's majesty?

MORTIMER.
She thinks on nothing now but present danger,
Nor looks to that which is so far removed.

MARY.
And fears she not the dread revenge of France?

MORTIMER.
With France she makes an everlasting peace;
And gives to Anjou's duke her throne and hand.

MARY.
Will not the King of Spain rise up in arms?

MORTIMER.
She fears not a collected world in arms?
If with her people she remains at peace.

MARY.
Were this a spectacle for British eyes?

MORTIMER.
This land, my queen, has, in these latter days,
Seen many a royal woman from the throne
Descend and mount the scaffold:--her own mother
And Catherine Howard trod this fatal path;
And was not Lady Grey a crowned head?

MARY (after a pause).
No, Mortimer, vain fears have blinded you;
'Tis but the honest care of your true heart,
Which conjures up these empty apprehensions.
It is not, sir, the scaffold that I fear:
There are so many still and secret means
By which her majesty of England may
Set all my claims to rest. Oh, trust me, ere

An executioner is found for me,
Assassins will be hired to do their work.
'Tis that which makes me tremble, Mortimer:
I never lift the goblet to my lips
Without an inward shuddering, lest the draught
May have been mingled by my sister's love.

MORTIMER.
No:--neither open or disguised murder
Shall e'er prevail against you:--fear no more;
All is prepared;--twelve nobles of the land
Are my confederates, and have pledged to-day,
Upon the sacrament, their faith to free you,
With dauntless arm, from this captivity.
Count Aubespine, the French ambassador,
Knows of our plot, and offers his assistance:
'Tis in his palace that we hold our meetings.

NARY.
You make me tremble, sir, but not for joy!
An evil boding penetrates my heart.
Know you, then, what you risk? Are you not scared
By Babington and Tichburn's bloody heads,
Set up as warnings upon London's bridge?
Nor by the ruin of those many victims
Who have, in such attempts, found certain death,
And only made my chains the heavier?
Fly hence, deluded, most unhappy youth!
Fly, if there yet be time for you, before
That crafty spy, Lord Burleigh, track your schemes,
And mix his traitors in your secret plots.
Fly hence:--as yet, success hath never smiled
On Mary Stuart's champions.

MORTIMER.
>I am not scared
By Babington and Tichburn's bloody heads
Set up as warnings upon London's bridge;
Nor by the ruin of those many victims
Who have, in such attempts, found certain death:
They also found therein immortal honor,
And death, in rescuing you, is dearest bliss.

MARY.
It is in vain: nor force nor guile can save me:--
My enemies are watchful, and the power
Is in their hands. It is not Paulet only
And his dependent host; all England guards
My prison gates: Elizabeth's free will
Alone can open them.

MORTIMER.
>Expect not that.

MARY.
One man alone on earth can open them.

MORTIMER.
Oh, let me know his name!

MARY.
>Lord Leicester.

MORTIMER.
>He!

[Starts back in wonder.

The Earl of Leicester! Your most bloody foe,
The favorite of Elizabeth! through him----

MARY.
If I am to be saved at all, 'twill be
Through him, and him alone. Go to him, sir;
Freely confide in him: and, as a proof
You come from me, present this paper to him.

[She takes a paper from her bosom; MORTIMER draws back, and hesitates to take it.

It doth contain my portrait:--take it, sir;
I've borne it long about me; but your uncle's
Close watchfulness has cut me off from all
Communication with him;--you were sent
By my good angel.

[He takes it.

MORTIMER.
    Oh, my queen! Explain
This mystery.

MARY.
    Lord Leicester will resolve it.
Confide in him, and he'll confide in you.
Who comes?

KENNEDY (entering hastily).
    'Tis Paulet; and he brings with him

A nobleman from court.

MORTIMER.
    It is Lord Burleigh.
Collect yourself, my queen, and strive to hear
The news he brings with equanimity.

[He retires through a side door, and KENNEDY follows him.

SCENE VII.

Enter LORD BURLEIGH, and PAULET.

PAULET (to MARY).
You wished to-day assurance of your fate;
My Lord of Burleigh brings it to you now;
Hear it with resignation, as beseems you.

MARY.
I hope with dignity, as it becomes
My innocence, and my exalted station.

BURLEIGH.
I come deputed from the court of justice.

MARY.
Lord Burleigh lends that court his willing tongue,
Which was already guided by his spirit.

PAULET.
You speak as if no stranger to the sentence.

MARY.
Lord Burleigh brings it; therefore do I know it.

PAULET.
[It would become you better, Lady Stuart,
To listen less to hatred.

MARY.
         I but name
My enemy: I said not that I hate him.]
But to the matter, sir.

BURLEIGH.
         You have acknowledged
The jurisdiction of the two-and-forty.

MARY.
My lord, excuse me, if I am obliged
So soon to interrupt you. I acknowledged,
Say you, the competence of the commission?
I never have acknowledged it, my lord;
How could I so? I could not give away
My own prerogative, the intrusted rights
Of my own people, the inheritance
Of my own son, and every monarch's honor
[The very laws of England say I could not.]
It is enacted by the English laws
That every one who stands arraigned of crime
Shall plead before a jury of his equals:
Who is my equal in this high commission?
Kings only are my peers.

BURLEIGH.
>	But yet you heard
The points of accusation, answered them
Before the court----

MARY.
>	'Tis true, I was deceived
By Hatton's crafty counsel:--he advised me,
For my own honor, and in confidence
In my good cause, and my most strong defence,
To listen to the points of accusation,
And prove their falsehoods. This, my lord, I did
From personal respect for the lords' names,
Not their usurped charge, which I disclaim.

BURLEIGH.
Acknowledge you the court, or not, that is
Only a point of mere formality,
Which cannot here arrest the course of justice.
You breathe the air of England; you enjoy
The law's protection, and its benefits;
You therefore are its subject.

MARY.
>	Sir, I breathe
The air within an English prison walls:
Is that to live in England; to enjoy
Protection from its laws? I scarcely know
And never have I pledged my faith to keep them.
I am no member of this realm; I am
An independent, and a foreign queen.

BURLEIGH.

And do you think that the mere name of queen
Can serve you as a charter to foment
In other countries, with impunity,
This bloody discord? Where would be the state's
Security, if the stern sword of justice
Could not as freely smite the guilty brow
Of the imperial stranger as the beggar's?

MARY.
I do not wish to be exempt from judgment,
It is the judges only I disclaim.

BURLEIGH.
The judges? How now, madam? Are they then
Base wretches, snatched at hazard from the crowd?
Vile wranglers that make sale of truth and justice;
Oppression's willing hirelings, and its tools?
Are they not all the foremost of this land,
Too independent to be else than honest,
And too exalted not to soar above
The fear of kings, or base servility?
Are they not those who rule a generous people
In liberty and justice; men, whose names
I need but mention to dispel each doubt,
Each mean suspicion which is raised against them?
Stands not the reverend primate at their head,
The pious shepherd of his faithful people,
The learned Talbot, keeper of the seals,
And Howard, who commands our conquering fleets?
Say, then, could England's sovereign do more
Than, out of all the monarchy, elect
The very noblest, and appoint them judges
In this great suit? And were it probable

That party hatred could corrupt one heart;
Can forty chosen men unite to speak
A sentence just as passion gives command?

MARY (after a short pause).
I am struck dumb by that tongue's eloquence,
Which ever was so ominous to me.
And how shall I, a weak, untutored woman,
Cope with so subtle, learned an orator?
Yes truly; were these lords as you describe them,
I must be mute; my cause were lost indeed,
Beyond all hope, if they pronounce me guilty.
But, sir, these names, which you are pleased to praise,
These very men, whose weight you think will crush me,
I see performing in the history
Of these dominions very different parts:
I see this high nobility of England,
This grave majestic senate of the realm,
Like to an eastern monarch's vilest slaves,
Flatter my uncle Henry's sultan fancies:
I see this noble, reverend House of Lords,
Venal alike with the corrupted Commons,
Make statutes and annul them, ratify
A marriage and dissolve it, as the voice
Of power commands: to-day it disinherits,
And brands the royal daughters of the realm
With the vile name of bastards, and to-morrow
Crowns them as queens, and leads them to the throne.
I see them in four reigns, with pliant conscience,
Four times abjure their faith; renounce the pope
With Henry, yet retain the old belief;
Reform themselves with Edward; hear the mass
Again with Mary; with Elizabeth,

Who governs now, reform themselves again.

BURLEIGH.
You say you are not versed in England's laws,
You seem well read, methinks, in her disasters.

MARY.
And these men are my judges?
   [As LORD BURLEIGH seems to wish to speak.
       My lord treasurer,
Towards you I will be just, be you but just
To me. 'Tis said that you consult with zeal
The good of England, and of England's queen;
Are honest, watchful, indefatigable;
I will believe it. Not your private ends,
Your sovereign and your country's weal alone,
Inspire your counsels and direct your deeds.
Therefore, my noble lord, you should the more
Distrust your heart; should see that you mistake not
The welfare of the government for justice.
I do not doubt, besides yourself, there are
Among my judges many upright men:
But they are Protestants, are eager all
For England's quiet, and they sit in judgment
On me, the Queen of Scotland, and the papist.
It is an ancient saying, that the Scots
And England to each other are unjust;
And hence the rightful custom that a Scot
Against an Englishman, or Englishman
Against a Scot, cannot be heard in judgment.
Necessity prescribed this cautious law;
Deep policy oft lies in ancient customs:
My lord, we must respect them. Nature cast

Into the ocean these two fiery nations
Upon this plank, and she divided it
Unequally, and bade them fight for it.
The narrow bed of Tweed alone divides
These daring spirits; often hath the blood
Of the contending parties dyed its waves.
Threatening, and sword in hand, these thousand years,
From both its banks they watch their rival's motions,
Most vigilant and true confederates,
With every enemy of the neighbor state.
No foe oppresses England, but the Scot
Becomes his firm ally; no civil war
Inflames the towns of Scotland, but the English
Add fuel to the fire: this raging hate
Will never be extinguished till, at last,
One parliament in concord shall unite them,
One common sceptre rule throughout the isle.

BURLEIGH.
And from a Stuart, then, should England hope
This happiness?

MARY.
     Oh! why should I deny it?
Yes, I confess, I cherished the fond hope;
I thought myself the happy instrument
To join in freedom, 'neath the olive's shade,
Two generous realms in lasting happiness!
I little thought I should become the victim
Of their old hate, their long-lived jealousy;
And the sad flames of that unhappy strife,
I hoped at last to smother, and forever:
And, as my ancestor, great Richmond, joined

The rival roses after bloody contest,
To join in peace the Scotch and English crowns.

BURLEIGH.
An evil way you took to this good end,
To set the realm on fire, and through the flames
Of civil war to strive to mount the throne.

MARY.
I wished not that:--I wished it not, by Heaven!
When did I strive at that? Where are your proofs?

BURLEIGH.
I came not hither to dispute; your cause
Is no more subject to a war of words.
The great majority of forty voices
Hath found that you have contravened the law
Last year enacted, and have now incurred
Its penalty.

   [Producing the verdict.

MARY.
    Upon this statute, then,
My lord, is built the verdict of my judges?

BURLEIGH (reading).
Last year it was enacted, "If a plot
Henceforth should rise in England, in the name
Or for the benefit of any claimant
To England's crown, that justice should be done
On such pretender, and the guilty party
Be prosecuted unto death." Now, since

It has been proved----

MARY.
     Lord Burleigh, I can well
Imagine that a law expressly aimed
At me, and framed to compass my destruction
May to my prejudice be used. Oh! Woe
To the unhappy victim, when the tongue
That frames the law shall execute the sentence.
Can you deny it, sir, that this same statute
Was made for my destruction, and naught else?

BURLEIGH.
It should have acted as a warning to you:
By your imprudence it became a snare.
You saw the precipice which yawned before you;
Yet, truly warned, you plunged into the deep.
With Babington, the traitor, and his bands
Of murderous companions, were you leagued.
You knew of all, and from your prison led
Their treasonous plottings with a deep-laid plan.

MARY.
When did I that, my lord? Let them produce
The documents.

BURLEIGH.
     You have already seen them
They were before the court, presented to you.

MARY.
Mere copies written by another hand;
Show me the proof that they were dictated

By me, that they proceeded from my lips,
And in those very terms in which you read them.

BURLEIGH.
Before his execution, Babington
Confessed they were the same which he received.

MARY.
Why was he in his lifetime not produced
Before my face? Why was he then despatched
So quickly that he could not be confronted
With her whom he accused?

BURLEIGH.
      Besides, my lady,
Your secretaries, Curl and Nau, declare
On oath, they are the very selfsame letters
Which from your lips they faithfully transcribed.

MARY.
And on my menials' testimony, then,
I am condemned; upon the word of those
Who have betrayed me, me, their rightful queen!
Who in that very moment, when they came
As witnesses against me, broke their faith!

BURLEIGH.
You said yourself, you held your countryman
To be an upright, conscientious man.

MARY.
I thought him such; but 'tis the hour of danger
Alone, which tries the virtue of a man.

[He ever was an honest man, but weak
In understanding; and his subtle comrade,
Whose faith, observe, I never answered for,
Might easily seduce him to write down
More than he should;] the rack may have compelled him
To say and to confess more than he knew.
He hoped to save himself by this false witness,
And thought it could not injure me--a queen.

BURLEIGH.
The oath he swore was free and unconstrained.

MARY.
But not before my face! How now, my lord?
The witnesses you name are still alive;
Let them appear against me face to face,
And there repeat what they have testified.
Why am I then denied that privilege,
That right which e'en the murderer enjoys?
I know from Talbot's mouth, my former keeper,
That in this reign a statute has been passed
Which orders that the plaintiff be confronted
With the defendant; is it so, good Paulet?
I e'er have known you as an honest man;
Now prove it to me; tell me, on your conscience,
If such a law exist or not in England?

PAULET.
Madam, there does: that is the law in England.
I must declare the truth.

MARY.
    Well, then, my lord,

If I am treated by the law of England
So hardly, when that law oppresses me,
Say, why avoid this selfsame country's law,
When 'tis for my advantage? Answer me;
Why was not Babington confronted with me?
Why not my servants, who are both alive?

BURLEIGH.
Be not so hasty, lady; 'tis not only
Your plot with Babington----

MARY.
      'Tis that alone
Which arms the law against me; that alone
From which I'm called upon to clear myself.
Stick to the point, my lord; evade it not.

BURLEIGH.
It has been proved that you have corresponded
With the ambassador of Spain, Mendoza----

MARY.
Stick to the point, my lord.

BURLEIGH.
      That you have formed
Conspiracies to overturn the fixed
Religion of the realm; that you have called
Into this kingdom foreign powers, and roused
All kings in Europe to a war with England.

MARY.
And were it so, my lord--though I deny it--

But e'en suppose it were so: I am kept
Imprisoned here against all laws of nations.
I came not into England sword in hand;
I came a suppliant; and at the hands
Of my imperial kinswoman I claimed
The sacred rights of hospitality,
When power seized upon me, and prepared
To rivet fetters where I hoped protection.
Say, is my conscience bound, then, to this realm?
What are the duties that I owe to England?
I should but exercise a sacred right,
Derived from sad necessity, if I
Warred with these bonds, encountered might with might,
Roused and incited every state in Europe
For my protection to unite in arms.
Whatever in a rightful war is just
And loyal, 'tis my right to exercise:
Murder alone, the secret, bloody deed,
My conscience and my pride alike forbid.
Murder would stain me, would dishonor me:
Dishonor me, my lord, but not condemn me,
Nor subject me to England's courts of law:
For 'tis not justice, but mere violence,
Which is the question 'tween myself and England.

BURLEIGH (significantly).
Talk not, my lady, of the dreadful right
Of power: 'tis seldom on the prisoner's side.

MARY.
I am the weak, she is the mighty one:
'Tis well, my lord; let her, then, use her power;
Let her destroy me; let me bleed, that she

May live secure; but let her, then, confess
That she hath exercised her power alone,
And not contaminate the name of justice.
Let her not borrow from the laws the sword
To rid her of her hated enemy;
Let her not clothe in this religious garb
The bloody daring of licentious might;
Let not these juggling tricks deceive the world.

[Returning the sentence.

Though she may murder me, she cannot judge me:
Let her no longer strive to join the fruits
Of vice with virtue's fair and angel show;
But let her dare to seem the thing she is.

[Exit.

SCENE VIII.

BURLEIGH, PAULET.

BURLEIGH.
She scorns us, she defies us! will defy us,
Even at the scaffold's foot. This haughty heart
Is not to be subdued. Say, did the sentence
Surprise her? Did you see her shed one tear,
Or even change her color? She disdains
To make appeal to our compassion. Well
She knows the wavering mind of England's queen.
Our apprehensions make her bold.

PAULET.
          My lord,
Take the pretext away which buoys it up,
And you shall see this proud defiance fail
That very moment. I must say, my lord,
Irregularities have been allowed
In these proceedings; Babington and Ballard
Should have been brought, with her two secretaries,
Before her, face to face.

BURLEIGH.
          No, Paulet, no.
That was not to be risked; her influence
Upon the human heart is too supreme;
Too strong the female empire of her tears.
Her secretary, Curl, if brought before her,
And called upon to speak the weighty word
On which her life depends, would straight shrink back
And fearfully revoke his own confession.

PAULET.
Then England's enemies will fill the world
With evil rumors; and the formal pomp
Of these proceedings to the minds of all
Will only signalize an act of outrage.

BURLEIGH.
That is the greatest torment of our queen,
[That she can never 'scape the blame. Oh God!]
Had but this lovely mischief died before
She set her faithless foot on English ground.

PAULET.
Amen, say I!

BURLEIGH.
    Had sickness but consumed her!

PAULET.
England had been secured from such misfortune.

BURLEIGH.
And yet, if she had died in nature's course,
The world would still have called us murderers.

PAULET.
'Tis true, the world will think, despite of us,
Whate'er it list.

BURLEIGH.
    Yet could it not be proved?
And it would make less noise.

PAULET.
    Why, let it make
What noise it may. It is not clamorous blame,
'Tis righteous censure only which can wound.

BURLEIGH.
We know that holy justice cannot 'scape
The voice of censure; and the public cry
Is ever on the side of the unhappy:
Envy pursues the laurelled conqueror;
The sword of justice, which adorns the man,

Is hateful in a woman's hand; the world
Will give no credit to a woman's justice
If woman be the victim. Vain that wo,
The judges, spoke what conscience dictated;
She has the royal privilege of mercy;
She must exert it: 'twere not to be borne,
Should she let justice take its full career.

PAULET.
And therefore----

BURLEIGH.
      Therefore should she live? Oh, no,
She must not live; it must not be. 'Tis this,
Even this, my friend, which so disturbs the queen,
And scares all slumber from her couch; I read
Her soul's distracting contest in her eyes:
She fears to speak her wishes, yet her looks,
Her silent looks, significantly ask,
"Is there not one amongst my many servants
To save me from this sad alternative?
Either to tremble in eternal fear
Upon my throne, or else to sacrifice
A queen of my own kindred on the block?"

PAULET.
'Tis even so; nor can it be avoided----

BURLEIGH.
Well might it be avoided, thinks the queen,
If she had only more attentive servants.

PAULET.

How more attentive?

BURLEIGH.
        Such as could interpret
A silent mandate.

PAULET.
        What? A silent mandate!

BURLEIGH.
Who, when a poisonous adder is delivered
Into their hands, would keep the treacherous charge
As if it were a sacred, precious jewel?

PAULET.
A precious jewel is the queen's good name
And spotless reputation: good my lord,
One cannot guard it with sufficient care.

BURLEIGH.
When out of Shrewsbury's hands the Queen of Scots
Was trusted to Sir Amias Paulet's care,
The meaning was----

PAULET.
        I hope to God, my lord,
The meaning was to give the weightiest charge
Into the purest hands; my lord, my lord!
By heaven I had disdained this bailiff's office
Had I not thought the service claimed the care
Of the best man that England's realm can boast.
Let me not think I am indebted for it
To anything but my unblemished name.

BURLEIGH.
Spread the report she wastes; grows sicker still
And sicker; and expires at last in peace;
Thus will she perish in the world's remembrance,
And your good name is pure.

PAULET.
       But not my conscience.

BURLEIGH.
Though you refuse us, sir, your own assistance,
You will not sure prevent another's hand.

PAULET.
No murderer's foot shall e'er approach her threshold
Whilst she's protected by my household gods.
Her life's a sacred trust; to me the head
Of Queen Elizabeth is not more sacred.
Ye are the judges; judge, and break the staff;
And when 'tis time then let the carpenter
With axe and saw appear to build the scaffold.
My castle's portals shall be open to him,
The sheriff and the executioners:
Till then she is intrusted to my care;
And be assured I will fulfil my trust,
She shall nor do nor suffer what's unjust.

       [Exeunt.

ACT II.

SCENE I.

London, a Hall in the Palace of Westminster. The EARL OF KENT and SIR WILLIAM DAVISON meeting.

DAVISON.
Is that my Lord of Kent? So soon returned?
Is then the tourney, the carousal over?

KENT.
How now? Were you not present at the tilt?

DAVISON.
My office kept me here.

KENT.
        Believe me, sir,
You've lost the fairest show which ever state
Devised, or graceful dignity performed:
For beauty's virgin fortress was presented
As by desire invested; the Earl-Marshal,
The Lord-High Admiral, and ten other knights
Belonging to the queen defended it,
And France's cavaliers led the attack.
A herald marched before the gallant troop,

And summoned, in a madrigal, the fortress;
And from the walls the chancellor replied;
And then the artillery was played, and nosegays
Breathing delicious fragrance were discharged
From neat field-pieces; but in vain, the storm
Was valiantly resisted, and desire
Was forced, unwillingly, to raise the siege.

DAVISON.
A sign of evil-boding, good my lord,
For the French Suitors.

KENT.
    Why, you know that this
Was but in sport; when the attack's in earnest
The fortress will, no doubt, capitulate.

DAVISON.
Ha! think you so? I never can believe it.

KENT.
The hardest article of all is now
Adjusted and acceded to by France;
The Duke of Anjou is content to hold
His holy worship in a private chapel;
And openly he promises to honor
And to protect the realm's established faith.
Had ye but heard the people's joyful shouts
Where'er the tidings spread, for it has been
The country's constant fear the queen might die
Without immediate issue of her body;
And England bear again the Romish chains
If Mary Stuart should ascend the throne.

DAVISON.
This fear appears superfluous; she goes
Into the bridal chamber; Mary Stuart
Enters the gates of death.

KENT.
>	The queen approaches.

SCENE II.

Enter ELIZABETH, led in by LEICESTER, COUNT AUBESPINE, BELLIEVRE, LORDS SHREWSBURY and BURLEIGH, with other French and English gentlemen.

ELIZABETH (to AUBESPINE).
Count, I am sorry for these noblemen
Whose gallant zeal hath brought them over sea
To visit these our shores, that they, with us,
Must miss the splendor of St. Germain's court.
Such pompous festivals of godlike state
I cannot furnish as the royal court
Of France. A sober and contented people,
Which crowd around me with a thousand blessings
Whene'er in public I present myself:
This is the spectacle which I can show,
And not without some pride, to foreign eyes.
The splendor of the noble dames who bloom
In Catherine's beauteous garden would, I know,
Eclipse myself, and my more modest merits.

AUBESPINE.
The court of England has one lady only
To show the wondering foreigner; but all
That charms our hearts in the accomplished sex
Is seen united in her single person.

BELLIEVRE.
Great majesty of England, suffer us
To take our leave, and to our royal master,
The Duke of Anjou, bring the happy news.
The hot impatience of his heart would not
Permit him to remain at Paris; he
At Amiens awaits the joyful tidings;
And thence to Calais reach his posts to bring
With winged swiftness to his tranced ear
The sweet consent which, still we humbly hope,
Your royal lips will graciously pronounce.

ELIZABETH.
Press me no further now, Count Bellievre.
It is not now a time, I must repeat,
To kindle here the joyful marriage torch.
The heavens lower black and heavy o'er this land;
And weeds of mourning would become me better
Than the magnificence of bridal robes.
A fatal blow is aimed against my heart;
A blow which threatens to oppress my house.

BELLIEVRE.
We only ask your majesty to promise
Your royal hand when brighter days shall come.

ELIZABETH.

Monarchs are but the slaves of their condition;
They dare not hear the dictates of their hearts;
My wish was ever to remain unmarried,
And I had placed my greatest pride in this,
That men hereafter on my tomb might read,
"Here rests the virgin queen." But my good subjects
Are not content that this should be: they think,
E'en now they often think upon the time
When I shall be no more. 'Tis not enough
That blessings now are showered upon this land;
They ask a sacrifice for future welfare,
And I must offer up my liberty,
My virgin liberty, my greatest good,
To satisfy my people. Thus they'd force
A lord and master on me. 'Tis by this
I see that I am nothing but a woman
In their regard; and yet methought that I
Had governed like a man, and like a king.
Well wot I that it is not serving God
To quit the laws of nature; and that those
Who here have ruled before me merit praise,
That they have oped the cloister gates, and given
Thousands of victims of ill-taught devotion
Back to the duties of humanity.
But yet a queen who hath not spent her days
In fruitless, idle contemplation; who,
Without murmur, indefatigably
Performs the hardest of all duties; she
Should be exempted from that natural law
Which doth ordain one half of human kind
Shall ever be subservient to the other.

AUBESPINE.

Great queen, you have upon your throne done honor
To every virtue; nothing now remains
But to the sex, whose greatest boast you are
To be the leading star, and give the great
Example of its most consistent duties.
'Tis true, the man exists not who deserves
That you to him should sacrifice your freedom;
Yet if a hero's soul, descent, and rank,
And manly beauty can make mortal man
Deserving of this honor----

ELIZABETH.
      Without doubt,
My lord ambassador, a marriage union
With France's royal son would do me honor;
Yes, I acknowledge it without disguise,
If it must be, if I cannot prevent it,
If I must yield unto my people's prayers,
And much I fear they will o'erpower me,
I do not know in Europe any prince
To whom with less reluctance I would yield
My greatest treasure, my dear liberty.
Let this confession satisfy your master.

BELLIEVRE.
It gives the fairest hope, and yet it gives
Nothing but hope; my master wishes more.

ELIZABETH.
What wishes he?
  [She takes a ring from her finger, and thoughtfully examines it.
    In this a queen has not
One privilege above all other women.

This common token marks one common duty,
One common servitude; the ring denotes
Marriage, and 'tis of rings a chain is formed.
Convey this present to his highness; 'tis
As yet no chain, it binds me not as yet,
But out of it may grow a link to bind me.

BELLIEVRE (kneeling).
This present, in his name, upon my knees,
I do receive, great queen, and press the kiss
Of homage on the hand of her who is
Henceforth my princess.

ELIZABETH (to the EARL OF LEICESTER, whom she, during the last speeches,
   had continually regarded).
      By your leave, my lord.

[She takes the blue ribbon from his neck [1], and invests Bellievre
with it.

Invest his highness with this ornament,
As I invest you with it, and receive you
Into the duties of my gallant order.
And, "Honi soit qui mal y pense." Thus perish
All jealousy between our several realms,
And let the bond of confidence unite
Henceforth, the crowns of Britain and of France.

BELLIEVRE.
Most sovereign queen, this is a day of joy;
Oh that it could be so for all, and no
Afflicted heart within this island mourn.

See! mercy beams upon thy radiant brow;
Let the reflection of its cheering light
Fall on a wretched princess, who concerns
Britain and France alike.

ELIZABETH.
          No further, count!
Let us not mix two inconsistent things;
If France be truly anxious for my hand,
It must partake my interests, and renounce
Alliance with my foes.

AUBESPINE.
          In thine own eyes
Would she not seem to act unworthily,
If in this joyous treaty she forgot
This hapless queen, the widow of her king;
In whose behalf her honor and her faith
Are bound to plead for grace.

ELIZABETH.
          Thus urged, I know
To rate this intercession at its worth;
France has discharged her duties as a friend,
I will fulfil my own as England's queen.

  [She bows to the French ambassadors, who, with the other
  gentlemen, retire respectfully.

[1] Till the time of Charles the First, the Knights of the Garter wore the blue ribbon with the George about their necks, as they still do the collars, on great days.--TRANSLATOR.

SCENE III.

Enter BURLEIGH, LEICESTER, and TALBOT.
The QUEEN takes her seat.

BURLEIGH.
Illustrious sovereign, thou crown'st to-day
The fervent wishes of thy people; now
We can rejoice in the propitious days
Which thou bestowest upon us; and we look
No more with fear and trembling towards the time
Which, charged with storms, futurity presented.
Now, but one only care disturbs this land;
It is a sacrifice which every voice
Demands; Oh! grant but this and England's peace
Will be established now and evermore.

ELIZABETH.
What wish they still, my lord? Speak.

BURLEIGH.
      They demand
The Stuart's head. If to thy people thou
Wouldst now secure the precious boon of freedom,
And the fair light of truth so dearly won,
Then she must die; if we are not to live
In endless terror for thy precious life
The enemy must fall; for well thou know'st
That all thy Britons are not true alike;
Romish idolatry has still its friends

In secret, in this island, who foment
The hatred of our enemies. Their hearts
All turn toward this Stuart; they are leagued
With the two plotting brothers of Lorrain,
The foes inveterate of thy house and name.
'Gainst thee this raging faction hath declared
A war of desolation, which they wage
With the deceitful instruments of hell.
At Rheims, the cardinal archbishop's see,
There is the arsenal from which they dart
These lightnings; there the school of regicide;
Thence, in a thousand shapes disguised, are sent
Their secret missionaries to this isle;
Their bold and daring zealots; for from thence
Have we not seen the third assassin come?
And inexhausted is the direful breed
Of secret enemies in this abyss.
While in her castle sits at Fotheringay,
The Ate [1] of this everlasting war,
Who, with the torch of love, spreads flames around;
For her who sheds delusive hopes on all,
Youth dedicates itself to certain death;
To set her free is the pretence--the aim
Is to establish her upon the throne.
For this accursed House of Guise denies
Thy sacred right; and in their mouths thou art
A robber of the throne, whom chance has crowned.
By them this thoughtless woman was deluded,
Proudly to style herself the Queen of England;
No peace can be with her, and with her house;
[Their hatred is too bloody, and their crimes
Too great;] thou must resolve to strike, or suffer--
Her life is death to thee, her death thy life.

ELIZABETH.
My lord, you bear a melancholy office;
I know the purity which guides your zeal,
The solid wisdom which informs your speech;
And yet I hate this wisdom, when it calls
For blood, I hate it in my inmost soul.
Think of a milder counsel--Good my Lord
Of Shrewsbury, we crave your judgment here.

TALBOT.
[Desire you but to know, most gracious queen,
What is for your advantage, I can add
Nothing to what my lord high-treasurer
Has urged; then, for your welfare, let the sentence
Be now confirmed--this much is proved already:
There is no surer method to avert
The danger from your head and from the state.
Should you in this reject our true advice,
You can dismiss your council. We are placed
Here as your counsellors, but to consult
The welfare of this land, and with our knowledge
And our experience we are bound to serve you!
But in what's good and just, most gracious queen,
You have no need of counsellors, your conscience
Knows it full well, and it is written there.
Nay, it were overstepping our commission
If we attempted to instruct you in it.

ELIZABETH.
Yet speak, my worthy Lord of Shrewsbury,
'Tis not our understanding fails alone,
Our heart too feels it wants some sage advice.]

TALBOT.
Well did you praise the upright zeal which fires
Lord Burleigh's loyal breast; my bosom, too,
Although my tongue be not so eloquent,
Beats with no weaker, no less faithful pulse.
Long may you live, my queen, to be the joy
Of your delighted people, to prolong
Peace and its envied blessings in this realm.
Ne'er hath this isle beheld such happy days
Since it was governed by its native kings.
Oh, let it never buy its happiness
With its good name; at least, may Talbot's eyes
Be closed in death e'er this shall come to pass.

ELIZABETH.
Forbid it, heaven, that our good name be stained!

TALBOT.
Then must you find some other way than this
To save thy kingdom, for the sentence passed
Of death against the Stuart is unjust.
You cannot upon her pronounce a sentence
Who is not subject to you.

ELIZABETH.
     Then, it seems,
My council and my parliament have erred;
Each bench of justice in the land is wrong,
Which did with one accord admit this right.

TALBOT (after a pause).
The proof of justice lies not in the voice

Of numbers; England's not the world, nor is
Thy parliament the focus, which collects
The vast opinion of the human race.
This present England is no more the future
Than 'tis the past; as inclination changes,
Thus ever ebbs and flows the unstable tide
Of public judgment. Say not, then, that thou
Must act as stern necessity compels,
That thou must yield to the importunate
Petitions of thy people; every hour
Thou canst experience that thy will is free.
Make trial, and declare thou hatest blood,
And that thou wilt protect thy sister's life;
Show those who wish to give thee other counsels,
That here thy royal anger is not feigned,
And thou shalt see how stern necessity
Can vanish, and what once was titled justice
Into injustice be converted: thou
Thyself must pass the sentence, thou alone
Trust not to this unsteady, trembling reed,
But hear the gracious dictates of thy heart.
God hath not planted rigor in the frame
Of woman; and the founders of this realm,
Who to the female hand have not denied
The reins of government, intend by this
To show that mercy, not severity,
Is the best virtue to adorn a crown.

ELIZABETH.
Lord Shrewsbury is a fervent advocate
For mine and England's enemy; I must
Prefer those counsellors who wish my welfare.

TALBOT.
Her advocates have an invidious task!
None will, by speaking in her favor, dare
To meet thy anger: stiffer, then, an old
And faithful counsellor (whom naught on earth
Can tempt on the grave's brink) to exercise
The pious duty of humanity.
It never shall be said that, in thy council,
Passion and interest could find a tongue,
While mercy's pleading voice alone was mute.
All circumstances have conspired against her;
Thou ne'er hast seen her face, and nothing speaks
Within thy breast for one that's stranger to thee.
I do not take the part of her misdeeds;
They say 'twas she who planned her husband's murder:
'Tis true that she espoused his murderer.
A grievous crime, no doubt; but then it happened
In darksome days of trouble and dismay,
In the stern agony of civil war,
When she, a woman, helpless and hemmed in
By a rude crowd of rebel vassals, sought
Protection in a powerful chieftain's arms.
God knows what arts were used to overcome her!
For woman is a weak and fragile thing.

ELIZABETH.
Woman's not weak; there are heroic souls
Among the sex; and, in my presence, sir,
I do forbid to speak of woman's weakness.

TALBOT.
Misfortune was for thee a rigid school;
Thou wast not stationed on the sunny side

Of life; thou sawest no throne, from far, before thee;
The grave was gaping for thee at thy feet.
At Woodstock, and in London's gloomy tower,
'Twas there the gracious father of this land
Taught thee to know thy duty, by misfortune.
No flatterer sought thee there: there learned thy soul,
Far from the noisy world and its distractions,
To commune with itself, to think apart,
And estimate the real goods of life.
No God protected this poor sufferer:
Transplanted in her early youth to France,
The court of levity and thoughtless joys,
There, in the round of constant dissipation,
She never heard the earnest voice of truth;
She was deluded by the glare of vice,
And driven onward by the stream of ruin.
Hers was the vain possession of a face,
And she outshone all others of her sex
As far in beauty, as in noble birth.

ELIZABETH.
Collect yourself, my Lord of Shrewsbury;
Bethink you we are met in solemn council.
Those charms must surely be without compare,
Which can engender, in an elder's blood,
Such fire. My Lord of Leicester, you alone
Are silent; does the subject which has made
Him eloquent, deprive you of your speech?

LEICESTER.
Amazement ties my tongue, my queen, to think
That they should fill thy soul with such alarms,
And that the idle tales, which, in the streets,

Of London, terrify the people's ears,
Should reach the enlightened circle of thy council,
And gravely occupy our statesmen's minds.
Astonishment possesses me, I own,
To think this lackland Queen of Scotland, she
Who could not save her own poor throne, the jest
Of her own vassals, and her country's refuse,
[Who in her fairest days of freedom, was
But thy despised puppet,] should become
At once thy terror when a prisoner.
What, in Heaven's name, can make her formidable?
That she lays claim to England? that the Guises
Will not acknowledge thee as queen?
[Did then Thy people's loyal fealty await
These Guises' approbation?] Can these Guises,
With their objections, ever shake the right
Which birth hath given thee; which, with one consent,
The votes of parliament have ratified?
And is not she, by Henry's will, passed o'er
In silence? Is it probable that England,
As yet so blessed in the new light's enjoyment,
Should throw itself into this papist's arms?
From thee, the sovereign it adores, desert
To Darnley's murderess? What will they then,
These restless men, who even in thy lifetime
Torment thee with a successor; who cannot
Dispose of thee in marriage soon enough
To rescue church and state from fancied peril?
Stand'st thou not blooming there in youthful prime
While each step leads her towards the expecting tomb?
By Heavens, I hope thou wilt full many a year
Walk o'er the Stuart's grave, and ne'er become
Thyself the instrument of her sad end.

BURLEIGH.
Lord Leicester hath not always held this tone.

LEICESTER.
'Tis true, I in the court of justice gave
My verdict for her death; here, in the council,
I may consistently speak otherwise
Here, right is not the question, but advantage.
Is this a time to fear her power, when France,
Her only succor, has abandoned her?
When thou preparest with thy hand to bless
The royal son of France, when the fair hope
Of a new, glorious stem of sovereigns
Begins again to blossom in this land?
Why hasten then her death? She's dead already.
Contempt and scorn are death to her; take heed
Lest ill-timed pity call her into life.
'Tis therefore my advice to leave the sentence,
By which her life is forfeit, in full force.
Let her live on; but let her live beneath
The headsman's axe, and, from the very hour
One arm is lifted for her, let it fall.

ELIZABETH (rises).
My lords, I now have heard your several thoughts,
And give my ardent thanks for this your zeal.
With God's assistance, who the hearts of kings
Illumines, I will weigh your arguments,
And choose what best my judgment shall approve.

   [To BURLEIGH.

[Lord Burleigh's honest fears, I know it well,
Are but the offspring of his faithful care;
But yet, Lord Leicester has most truly said,
There is no need of haste; our enemy
Hath lost already her most dangerous sting--
The mighty arm of France: the fear that she
Might quickly be the victim of their zeal
Will curb the blind impatience of her friends.]

[1] The picture of Ate, the goddess of mischief, we are acquainted with from Homer, II. v. 91, 130. I. 501. She is a daughter of Jupiter, and eager to prejudice every one, even the immortal gods. She counteracted Jupiter himself, on which account he seized her by her beautiful hair, and hurled her from heaven to the earth, where she now, striding over the heads of men, excites them to evil in order to involve them in calamity.--HERDER.

Shakspeare has, in Julius Caesar, made a fine use of this image:--

"And Caesar's spirit ranging for revenge
with Ate by his side, come hot from hell,
Shall in these confines, with a monarch's voice,
Cry havoc, and let slip the dogs of war."

I need not point out to the reader the beautiful propriety of introducing the evil spirit on this occasion.--TRANSLATOR.

SCENE IV.

    Enter SIR AMIAS PAULET and MORTIMER.

ELIZABETH.
There's Sir Amias Paulet; noble sir,
What tidings bring you?

PAULET.
      Gracious sovereign,
My nephew, who but lately is returned
From foreign travel, kneels before thy feet,
And offers thee his first and earliest homage,
Grant him thy royal grace, and let him grow
And flourish in the sunshine of thy favor.

MORTIMER (kneeling on one knee).
Long live my royal mistress! Happiness
And glory from a crown to grace her brows!

ELIZABETH.
Arise, sir knight; and welcome here in England;
You've made, I hear, the tour, have been in France
And Rome, and tarried, too, some time at Rheims:
Tell me what plots our enemies are hatching?

MORTIMER.
May God confound them all! And may the darts
Which they shall aim against my sovereign,
Recoiling, strike their own perfidious breasts!

ELIZABETH.
Did you see Morgan, and the wily Bishop
Of Ross?

MORTIMER.
    I saw, my queen, all Scottish exiles
Who forge at Rheims their plots against this realm.
I stole into their confidence in hopes
To learn some hint of their conspiracies.

PAULET.
Private despatches they intrusted to him,
In cyphers, for the Queen of Scots, which he,
With loyal hand, hath given up to us.

ELIZABETH.
Say, what are then their latest plans of treason?

MORTIMER.
It struck them all as 'twere a thunderbolt,
That France should leave them, and with England close
This firm alliance; now they turn their hopes
Towards Spain----

ELIZABETH.
    This, Walsingham hath written us.

MORTIMER.
Besides, a bull, which from the Vatican
Pope Sixtus lately levelled at thy throne,
Arrived at Rheims, as I was leaving it;
With the next ship we may expect it here.

LEICESTER.
England no more is frightened by such arms.

BURLEIGH.
They're always dangerous in bigots' hands.

ELIZABETH (looking steadfastly at MORTIMER).
Your enemies have said that you frequented
The schools at Rheims, and have abjured your faith.

MORTIMER.
So I pretended, that I must confess;
Such was my anxious wish to serve my queen.

ELIZABETH (to PAULET, who presents papers to her).
What have you there?

PAULET.
    'Tis from the Queen of Scots.
'Tis a petition, and to thee addressed.

BURLEIGH (hastily catching at it).
Give me the paper.

PAULET (giving it to the QUEEN).
    By your leave, my lord
High-treasurer; the lady ordered me
To bring it to her majesty's own hands.
She says I am her enemy; I am
The enemy of her offences only,
And that which is consistent with my duty
I will, and readily, oblige her in.

[The QUEEN takes the letter: as she reads it MORTIMER
  and LEICESTER speak some words in private.

BURLEIGH (to PAULET).
What may the purport of the letter be?
Idle complaints, from which one ought to screen
The queen's too tender heart.

PAULET.
      What it contains
She did not hide from me; she asks a boon;
She begs to be admitted to the grace
Of speaking with the queen.

BURLEIGH.
      It cannot be.

TALBOT.
Why not? Her supplication's not unjust.

BURLEIGH.
For her, the base encourager of murder;
Her, who hath thirsted for our sovereign's blood,
The privilege to see the royal presence
Is forfeited: a faithful counsellor
Can never give this treacherous advice.

TALBOT.
And if the queen is gracious, sir, are you
The man to hinder pity's soft emotions?

BURLEIGH.
She is condemned to death; her head is laid
Beneath the axe, and it would ill become
The queen to see a death-devoted head.
The sentence cannot have its execution

If the queen's majesty approaches her,
For pardon still attends the royal presence,
As sickness flies the health-dispensing hand.

ELIZABETH (having read the letter, dries her tears).
Oh, what is man! What is the bliss of earth!
To what extremities is she reduced
Who with such proud and splendid hopes began!
Who, called to sit on the most ancient throne
Of Christendom, misled by vain ambition,
Hoped with a triple crown to deck her brows!
How is her language altered, since the time
When she assumed the arms of England's crown,
And by the flatterers of her court was styled
Sole monarch of the two Britannic isles!
Forgive me, lords, my heart is cleft in twain,
Anguish possesses me, and my soul bleeds
To think that earthly goods are so unstable,
And that the dreadful fate which rules mankind
Should threaten mine own house, and scowl so near me.

TALBOT.
Oh, queen! the God of mercy hath informed
Your heart; Oh! hearken to this heavenly guidance.
Most grievously, indeed, hath she atoned.
Her grievous crime, and it is time that now,
At last, her heavy penance have an end.
Stretch forth your hand to raise this abject queen,
And, like the luminous vision of an angel,
Descend into her gaol's sepulchral night.

BURLEIGH.
Be steadfast, mighty queen; let no emotion

Of seeming laudable humanity
Mislead thee; take not from thyself the power
Of acting as necessity commands.
Thou canst not pardon her, thou canst not save her:
Then heap not on thyself the odious blame,
That thou, with cruel and contemptuous triumph,
Didst glut thyself with gazing on thy victim.

LEICESTER.
Let us, my lords, remain within our bounds;
The queen is wise, and doth not need our counsels
To lead her to the most becoming choice.
This meeting of the queens hath naught in common
With the proceedings of the court of justice.
The law of England, not the monarch's will,
Condemns the Queen of Scotland, and 'twere worthy
Of the great soul of Queen Elizabeth,
To follow the soft dictates of her heart,
Though justice swerves not from its rigid path.

ELIZABETH.
Retire, my lords. We shall, perhaps, find means
To reconcile the tender claims of pity
With what necessity imposes on us.
And now retire.
   [The LORDS retire; she calls SIR EDWARD MORTIMER back.
      Sir Edward Mortimer!

SCENE V.

ELIZABETH, MORTIMER.

ELIZABETH (having measured him for some time with her eyes in silence).
You've shown a spirit of adventurous courage
And self-possession, far beyond your years.
He who has timely learnt to play so well
The difficult dissembler's needful task
Becomes a perfect man before his time,
And shortens his probationary years.
Fate calls you to a lofty scene of action;
I prophesy it, and can, happily
For you, fulfil, myself, my own prediction.

MORTIMER.
Illustrious mistress, what I am, and all
I can accomplish, is devoted to you.

ELIZABETH.
You've made acquaintance with the foes of England.
Their hate against me is implacable;
Their fell designs are inexhaustible.
As yet, indeed, Almighty Providence
Hath shielded me; but on my brows the crown
Forever trembles, while she lives who fans
Their bigot-zeal, and animates their hopes.

MORTIMER.
She lives no more, as soon as you command it.

ELIZABETH.
Oh, sir! I thought I saw my labors end,
And I am come no further than at first,
I wished to let the laws of England act,
And keep my own hands pure from blood's defilement.

The sentence is pronounced--what gain I by it?
It must be executed, Mortimer,
And I must authorize the execution.
The blame will ever light on me, I must
Avow it, nor can save appearances.
That is the worst----

MORTIMER.
      But can appearances
Disturb your conscience where the cause is just?

ELIZABETH.
You are unpractised in the world, sir knight;
What we appear, is subject to the judgment
Of all mankind, and what we are, of no man.
No one will be convinced that I am right:
I must take care that my connivance in
Her death be wrapped in everlasting doubt.
In deeds of such uncertain double visage
Safety lies only in obscurity.
Those measures are the worst that stand avowed;
What's not abandoned, is not wholly lost.

MORTIMER (seeking to learn her meaning).
Then it perhaps were best----

ELIZABETH (quick).
      Ay, surely 'twere
The best; Oh, sir, my better angel speaks
Through you;--go on then, worthy sir, conclude
You are in earnest, you examine deep,
Have quite a different spirit from your uncle.

MORTIMER (surprised).
Have you imparted then your wishes to him?

ELIZABETH.
I am sorry that I have.

MORTIMER.
      Excuse his age,
The old man is grown scrupulous; such bold
Adventures ask the enterprising heart
Of youth----

ELIZABETH.
And may I venture then on you----

MORTIMER.
My hand I'll lend thee; save then as thou canst
Thy reputation----

ELIZABETH.
    Yes, sir; if you could
But waken me some morning with this news
"Maria Stuart, your bloodthirsty foe,
Breathed yesternight her last"----

MORTIMER.
      Depend on me.

ELIZABETH.
When shall my head lie calmly down to sleep?

MORTIMER.
The next new moon will terminate thy fears.

ELIZABETH.
And be the selfsame happy day the dawn
Of your preferment--so God speed you, sir;
And be not hurt, if, chance, my thankfulness
Should wear the mask of darkness. Silence is
The happy suitor's god. The closest bonds,
The dearest, are the works of secrecy.

    [Exit.

SCENE VI.

    MORTIMER (alone).

Go, false, deceitful queen! As thou deludest
The world, e'en so I cozen thee; 'tis right,
Thus to betray thee; 'tis a worthy deed.
Look I then like a murderer? Hast thou read
Upon my brow such base dexterity?
Trust only to my arm, and keep thine own
Concealed--assume the pious outward show
Of mercy 'fore the world, while reckoning
In secret on my murderous aid; and thus
By gaining time we shall insure her rescue.
Thou wilt exalt me!--show'st me from afar
The costly recompense: but even were
Thyself the prize, and all thy woman's favor,
What art thou, poor one, and what canst thou proffer?
I scorn ambition's avaricious strife,
With her alone is all the charm of life,

O'er her, in rounds of endless glory, hover
Spirits with grace, and youth eternal blessed,
Celestial joy is throned upon her breast.
Thou hast but earthly, mortal goods to offer--
That sovereign good, for which all else be slighted,
When heart in heart, delighting and delighted;
Together flow in sweet forgetfulness;--
Ne'er didst thou woman's fairest crown possess,
Ne'er hast thou with thy hand a lover's heart requited.
I must attend Lord Leicester, and deliver
Her letter to him--'tis a hateful charge--
I have no confidence in this court puppet--
I can effect her rescue, I alone;
Be danger, honor, and the prize my own.

[As he is going, PAULET meets him.

SCENE VII.

MORTIMER, PAULET.

PAULET.
What said the queen to you?

MORTIMER.
  'Twas nothing, sir;
Nothing of consequence----

PAULET (looking at him earnestly).
  Hear, Mortimer!
It is a false and slippery ground on which

You tread. The grace of princes is alluring,
Youth loves ambition--let not yours betray you.

MORTIMER.
Was it not yourself that brought me to the court?

PAULET.
Oh, would to God I had not done as much!
The honor of our house was never reaped
In courts--stand fast, my nephew--purchase not
Too dear, nor stain your conscience with a crime.

MORTIMER.
What are these fears? What are you dreaming of?

PAULET.
How high soever the queen may pledge herself
To raise you, trust not her alluring words.
[The spirit of the world's a lying spirit,
And vice is a deceitful, treacherous friend.]
She will deny you, if you listen to her;
And, to preserve her own good name, will punish
The bloody deed, which she herself enjoined.

MORTIMER.
The bloody deed!----

PAULET.
    Away, dissimulation!--
I know the deed the queen proposed to you.
She hopes that your ambitious youth will prove
More docile than my rigid age. But say,
Have you then pledged your promise, have you?

MORTIMER.
Uncle!

PAULET.
   If you have done so, I abandon you,
And lay my curse upon you----

LEICESTER (entering).
        Worthy sir!
I with your nephew wish a word. The queen
Is graciously inclined to him; she wills
That to his custody the Scottish queen
Be with full powers intrusted. She relies
On his fidelity.

PAULET.
      Relies!--'tis well----

LEICESTER.
What say you, sir?

PAULET.
    Her majesty relies
On him; and I, my noble lord, rely
Upon myself, and my two open eyes.

      [Exit.

SCENE VIII.

LEICESTER, MORTIMER.

LEICESTER (surprised).
What ailed the knight?

MORTIMER.
     My lord, I cannot tell
What angers him: the confidence, perhaps,
The queen so suddenly confers on me.

LEICESTER.
Are you deserving then of confidence?

MORTIMER.
This would I ask of you, my Lord of Leicester.

LEICESTER.
You said you wished to speak with me in private.

MORTIMER.
Assure me first that I may safely venture.

LEICESTER.
Who gives me an assurance on your side?
Let not my want of confidence offend you;
I see you, sir, exhibit at this court
Two different aspects; one of them must be
A borrowed one; but which of them is real?

MORTIMER.
The selfsame doubts I have concerning you.

LEICESTER.

Which, then, shall pave the way to confidence?

MORTIMER.
He, who by doing it, is least in danger.

LEICESTER.
Well, that are you----

MORTIMER.
    No, you; the evidence
Of such a weighty, powerful peer as you
Can overwhelm my voice. My accusation
Is weak against your rank and influence.

LEICESTER.
Sir, you mistake. In everything but this
I'm powerful here; but in this tender point
Which I am called upon to trust you with,
I am the weakest man of all the court,
The poorest testimony can undo me.

MORTIMER.
If the all-powerful Earl of Leicester deign
To stoop so low to meet me, and to make
Such a confession to me, I may venture
To think a little better of myself,
And lead the way in magnanimity.

LEICESTER.
Lead you the way of confidence, I'll follow.

MORTIMER (producing suddenly the letter).
Here is a letter from the Queen of Scotland.

LEICESTER (alarmed, catches hastily at the letter).
Speak softly, sir! what see I? Oh, it is
Her picture!

   [Kisses and examines it with speechless joy--a pause.

MORTIMER (who has watched him closely the whole tine).
     Now, my lord, I can believe you.

LEICESTER (having hastily run through the letter).
You know the purport of this letter, sir.

MORTIMER.
Not I.

LEICESTER.
   Indeed! She surely hath informed you.

MORTIMER.
Nothing hath she informed me of. She said
You would explain this riddle to me--'tis
To me a riddle, that the Earl of Leicester,
The far-famed favorite of Elizabeth,
The open, bitter enemy of Mary,
And one of those who spoke her mortal sentence,
Should be the man from whom the queen expects
Deliverance from her woes; and yet it must be;
Your eyes express too plainly what your heart
Feels for the hapless lady.

LEICESTER.
           Tell me, Sir,

First, how it comes that you should take so warm
An interest in her fate; and what it was
Gained you her confidence?

MORTIMER.
          My lord, I can,
And in few words, explain this mystery.
I lately have at Rome abjured my creed,
And stand in correspondence with the Guises.
A letter from the cardinal archbishop
Was my credential with the Queen of Scots.

LEICESTER.
I am acquainted, sir, with your conversion;
'Twas that which waked my confidence towards you.
[Each remnant of distrust be henceforth banished;]
Your hand, sir, pardon me these idle doubts,
I cannot use too much precaution here.
Knowing how Walsingham and Burleigh hate me,
And, watching me, in secret spread their snares;
You might have been their instrument, their creature
To lure me to their toils.

MORTIMER.
          How poor a part
So great a nobleman is forced to play
At court! My lord, I pity you.

LEICESTER.
          With joy
I rest upon the faithful breast of friendship,
Where I can ease me of this long constraint.
You seem surprised, sir, that my heart is turned

So suddenly towards the captive queen.
In truth, I never hated her; the times
Have forced me to be her enemy.
She was, as you well know, my destined bride,
Long since, ere she bestowed her hand on Darnley,
While yet the beams of glory round her smiled,
Coldly I then refused the proffered boon.
Now in confinement, at the gates of death,
I claim her at the hazard of my life.

MORTIMER.
True magnanimity, my lord.

LEICESTER.
      The state
Of circumstances since that time is changed.
Ambition made me all insensible
To youth and beauty. Mary's hand I held
Too insignificant for me; I hoped
To be the husband of the Queen of England.

MORTIMER.
It is well known she gave you preference
Before all others.

LEICESTER.
      So, indeed, it seemed.
Now, after ten lost years of tedious courtship
And hateful self-constraint--oh, sir, my heart
Must ease itself of this long agony.
They call me happy! Did they only know
What the chains are, for which they envy me!
When I had sacrificed ten bitter years

To the proud idol of her vanity;
Submitted with a slave's humility
To every change of her despotic fancies
The plaything of each little wayward whim.
At times by seeming tenderness caressed,
As oft repulsed with proud and cold disdain;
Alike tormented by her grace and rigor:
Watched like a prisoner by the Argus eyes
Of jealousy; examined like a schoolboy,
And railed at like a servant. Oh, no tongue
Can paint this hell.

MORTIMER.
    My lord, I feel for you.

LEICESTER.
To lose, and at the very goal, the prize
Another comes to rob me of the fruits
Of my so anxious wooing. I must lose
To her young blooming husband all those rights
Of which I was so long in full possession;
And I must from the stage descend, where I
So long have played the most distinguished part.
'Tis not her hand alone this envious stranger
Threatens, he'd rob me of her favor too;
She is a woman, and he formed to please.

MORTIMER.
He is the son of Catherine. He has learnt
In a good school the arts of flattery.

LEICESTER.
Thus fall my hopes; I strove to seize a plank

To bear me in this shipwreck of my fortunes,
And my eye turned itself towards the hope
Of former days once more; then Mary's image
Within me was renewed, and youth and beauty
Once more asserted all their former rights.
No more 'twas cold ambition; 'twas my heart
Which now compared, and with regret I felt
The value of the jewel I had lost.
With horror I beheld her in the depths.
Of misery, cast down by my transgression;
Then waked the hope in me that I might still
Deliver and possess her; I contrived
To send her, through a faithful hand, the news
Of my conversion to her interests;
And in this letter which you brought me, she
Assures me that she pardons me, and offers
Herself as guerdon if I rescue her.

MORTIMER.
But you attempted nothing for her rescue.
You let her be condemned without a word:
You gave, yourself, your verdict for her death;
A miracle must happen, and the light
Of truth must move me, me, her keeper's nephew,
And heaven must in the Vatican at Rome
Prepare for her an unexpected succour,
Else had she never found the way to you.

LEICESTER.
Oh, sir, it has tormented me enough!
About this time it was that they removed her
From Talbot's castle, and delivered her
Up to your uncle's stricter custody.

Each way to her was shut. I was obliged
Before the world to persecute her still;
But do not think that I would patiently
Have seen her led to death. No, Sir; I hoped,
And still I hope, to ward off all extremes,
Till I can find some certain means to save her.

MORTIMER.
These are already found: my Lord of Leicester;
Your generous confidence in me deserves
A like return. I will deliver her.
That is my object here; my dispositions
Are made already, and your powerful aid
Assures us of success in our attempt.

LEICESTER.
What say you? You alarm me! How? You would----

MORTIMER.
I'll open forcibly her prison-gates;
I have confederates, and all is ready.

LEICESTER.
You have confederates, accomplices?
Alas! In what rash enterprise would you
Engage me? And these friends, know they my secret?

MORTIMER.
Fear not; our plan was laid without your help,
Without your help it would have been accomplished,
Had she not signified her resolution
To owe her liberty to you alone.

LEICESTER.
And can you, then, with certainty assure me
That in your plot my name has not been mentioned?

MORTIMER.
You may depend upon it. How, my lord,
So scrupulous when help is offered you?
You wish to rescue Mary, and possess her;
You find confederates; sudden, unexpected,
The readiest means fall, as it were from Heaven,
Yet you show more perplexity than joy.

LEICESTER.
We must avoid all violence; it is
Too dangerous an enterprise.

MORTIMER.
  Delay
Is also dangerous.

LEICESTER.
  I tell you, Sir,
'Tis not to be attempted----

MORTIMER.
  My lord,
Too hazardous for you, who would possess her;
But we, who only wish to rescue her,
We are more bold.

LEICESTER.
  Young man, you are too hasty
In such a thorny, dangerous attempt.

MORTIMER.
And you too scrupulous in honor's cause.

LEICESTER.
I see the trammels that are spread around us.

MORTIMER.
And I feel courage to break through them all.

LEICESTER.
Foolhardiness and madness, is this courage?

MORTIMER.
This prudence is not bravery, my lord.

LEICESTER.
You surely wish to end like Babington.

MORTIMER.
You not to imitate great Norfolk's virtue.

LEICESTER.
Norfolk ne'er won the bride he wooed so fondly.

MORTIMER.
But yet he proved how truly he deserved her.

LEICESTER.
If we are ruined, she must fall with us.

MORTIMER.
If we risk nothing, she will ne'er be rescued.

LEICESTER.
You will not weigh the matter, will not hear;
With blind and hasty rashness you destroy
The plans which I so happily had framed.

MORTIMER.
And what were then the plans which you had framed?
What have you done then to deliver her?
And how, if I were miscreant enough
To murder her, as was proposed to me
This moment by Elizabeth, and which
She looks upon as certain; only name
The measures you have taken to protect her?

LEICESTER.
Did the queen give you, then, this bloody order?

MORTIMER.
She was deceived in me, as Mary is in you.

LEICESTER.
And have you promised it? Say, have you?

MORTIMER.
That she might not engage another's hand,
I offered mine.

LEICESTER.
        Well done, sir; that was right;
This gives us leisure, for she rests secure
Upon your bloody service, and the sentence
Is unfulfilled the while, and we gain time.

MORTIMER (angrily).
No, we are losing time.

LEICESTER.
      The queen depends
On you, and will the readier make a show
Of mercy; and I may prevail on her
To give an audience to her adversary;
And by this stratagem we tie her hands
Yes! I will make the attempt, strain every nerve.

MORTIMER.
And what is gained by this? When she discovers
That I am cheating her, that Mary lives;
Are we not where we were? She never will
Be free; the mildest doom which can await her
At best is but perpetual confinement.
A daring deed must one day end the matter;
Why will you not with such a deed begin?
The power is in your hands, would you but rouse
The might of your dependents round about
Your many castles, 'twere an host; and still
Has Mary many secret friends. The Howards
And Percies' noble houses, though their chiefs
Be fallen, are rich in heroes; they but wait
For the example of some potent lord.
Away with feigning--act an open part,
And, like a loyal knight, protect your fair;
Fight a good fight for her! You know you are
Lord of the person of the Queen of England,
Whene'er you will: invite her to your castle,
Oft hath she thither followed you--then show

That you're a man; then speak as master; keep her
Confined till she release the Queen of Scots.

LEICESTER.
I am astonished--I am terrified!
Where would your giddy madness hurry you?
Are you acquainted with this country? Know you
The deeps and shallows of this court? With what
A potent spell this female sceptre binds
And rules men's spirits round her? 'Tis in vain
You seek the heroic energy which once
Was active in this land! it is subdued,
A woman holds it under lock and key,
And every spring of courage is relaxed.
Follow my counsel--venture nothing rashly.
Some one approaches-go----

MORTIMER.
    And Mary hopes--
Shall I return to her with empty comfort?

LEICESTER.
Bear her my vows of everlasting love.

MORTIMER.
Bear them yourself! I offered my assistance
As her deliverer, not your messenger.

    [Exit.

SCENE IX.

ELIZABETH, LEICESTER.

ELIZABETH.
Say, who was here? I heard the sound of voices.

LEICESTER (turning quickly and perplexed round on hearing the QUEEN).
It was young Mortimer----

ELIZABETH.
    How now, my lord:
Why so confused?

LEICESTER (collecting himself).
    Your presence is the cause.
Ne'er did I see thy beauty so resplendent,
My sight is dazzled by thy heavenly charms.
Oh!

ELIZABETH.
  Whence this sigh?

LEICESTER.
    Have I no reason, then,
To sigh? When I behold you in your glory,
I feel anew, with pain unspeakable,
The loss which threatens me.

ELIZABETH.
    What loss, my lord?

LEICESTER.
Your heart; your own inestimable self

Soon will you feel yourself within the arms
Of your young ardent husband, highly blessed;
He will possess your heart without a rival.
He is of royal blood, that am not I.
Yet, spite of all the world can say, there lives not
One on this globe who with such fervent zeal
Adores you as the man who loses you.
Anjou hath never seen you, can but love
Your glory and the splendor of your reign;
But I love you, and were you born of all
The peasant maids the poorest, I the first
Of kings, I would descend to your condition,
And lay my crown and sceptre at your feet!

ELIZABETH.
Oh, pity me, my Dudley; do not blame me;
I cannot ask my heart. Oh, that had chosen
Far otherwise! Ah, how I envy others
Who can exalt the object of their love!
But I am not so blest: 'tis not my fortune
To place upon the brows of him, the dearest
Of men to me, the royal crown of England.
The Queen of Scotland was allowed to make
Her hand the token of her inclination;
She hath had every freedom, and hath drunk,
Even to the very dregs, the cup of joy.

LEICESTER.
And now she drinks the bitter cup of sorrow.

ELIZABETH.
She never did respect the world's opinion;
Life was to her a sport; she never courted

The yoke to which I bowed my willing neck.
And yet, methinks, I had as just a claim
As she to please myself and taste the joys
Of life: but I preferred the rigid duties
Which royalty imposed on me; yet she,
She was the favorite of all the men
Because she only strove to be a woman;
And youth and age became alike her suitors.
Thus are the men voluptuaries all!
The willing slaves of levity and pleasure;
Value that least which claims their reverence.
And did not even Talbot, though gray-headed,
Grow young again when speaking of her charms?

LEICESTER.
Forgive him, for he was her keeper once,
And she has fooled him with her cunning wiles.

ELIZABETH.
And is it really true that she's so fair?
So often have I been obliged to hear
The praises of this wonder--it were well
If I could learn on what I might depend:
Pictures are flattering, and description lies;
I will trust nothing but my own conviction.
Why gaze you at me thus?

LEICESTER.
    I placed in thought
You and Maria Stuart side by side.
Yes! I confess I oft have felt a wish,
If it could be but secretly contrived,
To see you placed beside the Scottish queen,

Then would you feel, and not till then, the full
Enjoyment of your triumph: she deserves
To be thus humbled; she deserves to see,
With her own eyes, and envy's glance is keen,
Herself surpassed, to feel herself o'ermatched,
As much by thee in form and princely grace
As in each virtue that adorns the sex.

ELIZABETH.
In years she has the advantage----

LEICESTER.
            Has she so?
I never should have thought it. But her griefs,
Her sufferings, indeed! 'tis possible
Have brought down age upon her ere her time.
Yes, and 'twould mortify her more to see thee
As bride--she hath already turned her back
On each fair hope of life, and she would see thee
Advancing towards the open arms of joy.
See thee as bride of France's royal son,
She who hath always plumed herself so high
On her connection with the house of France,
And still depends upon its mighty aid.

ELIZABETH (with a careless air).
I'm teazed to grant this interview.

LEICESTER.
            She asks it
As a favor; grant it as a punishment.
For though you should conduct her to the block,
Yet would it less torment her than to see

Herself extinguished by your beauty's splendor.
Thus can you murder her as she hath wished
To murder you. When she beholds your beauty,
Guarded by modesty, and beaming bright,
In the clear glory of unspotted fame
(Which she with thoughtless levity discarded),
Exalted by the splendor of the crown,
And blooming now with tender bridal graces--
Then is the hour of her destruction come.
Yes--when I now behold you--you were never,
No, never were you so prepared to seal
The triumph of your beauty. As but now
You entered the apartment, I was dazzled
As by a glorious vision from on high.
Could you but now, now as you are, appear
Before her, you could find no better moment.

ELIZABETH.
Now? no, not now; no, Leicester; this must be
Maturely weighed--I must with Burleigh----

LEICESTER.
   Burleigh!
To him you are but sovereign, and as such
Alone he seeks your welfare; but your rights,
Derived from womanhood, this tender point
Must be decided by your own tribunal,
Not by the statesman; yet e'en policy
Demands that you should see her, and allure
By such a generous deed the public voice.
You can hereafter act as it may please you,
To rid you of the hateful enemy.

ELIZABETH.
But would it then become me to behold
My kinswoman in infamy and want?
They say she is not royally attended;
Would not the sight of her distress reproach me?

LEICESTER.
You need not cross her threshold; hear my counsel.
A fortunate conjuncture favors it.
The hunt you mean to honor with your presence
Is in the neighborhood of Fotheringay;
Permission may be given to Lady Stuart
To take the air; you meet her in the park,
As if by accident; it must not seem
To have been planned, and should you not incline,
You need not speak to her.

ELIZABETH.
    If I am foolish,
Be yours the fault, not mine. I would not care
To-day to cross your wishes; for to-day
I've grieved you more than all my other subjects.
  [Tenderly.
Let it then be your fancy. Leicester, hence
You see the free obsequiousness of love.
Which suffers that which it cannot approve.

  [LEICESTER prostrates himself before her, and the curtain falls.

ACT III.

SCENE I.

In a park. In the foreground trees; in the background
a distant prospect.

MARY advances, running from behind the trees.
HANNAH KENNEDY follows slowly.

KENNEDY.
You hasten on as if endowed with wings;
I cannot follow you so swiftly; wait.

MARY.
Freedom returns! Oh let me enjoy it.
Let me be childish; be thou childish with me.
Freedom invites me! Oh, let me employ it
Skimming with winged step light o'er the lea;
Have I escaped from this mansion of mourning?
Holds me no more the sad dungeon of care?
Let me, with joy and with eagerness burning,
Drink in the free, the celestial air.

KENNEDY.
Oh, my dear lady! but a very little
Is your sad gaol extended; you behold not

The wall that shuts us in; these plaited tufts
Of trees hide from your sight the hated object.

MARY.
Thanks to these friendly trees, that hide from me
My prison walls, and flatter my illusion!
Happy I now may deem myself, and free;
Why wake me from my dream's so sweet confusion?
The extended vault of heaven around me lies,
Free and unfettered range my wandering eyes
O'er space's vast, immeasurable sea!
From where yon misty mountains rise on high
I can my empire's boundaries explore;
And those light clouds which, steering southwards, fly,
Seek the mild clime of France's genial shore.
   Fast fleeting clouds! ye meteors that fly;
   Could I but with you sail through the sky!
   Tenderly greet the dear land of my youth!
   Here I am captive! oppressed by my foes,
   No other than you may carry my woes.
   Free through the ether your pathway is seen,
   Ye own not the power of this tyrant queen.

KENNEDY.
Alas! dear lady! You're beside yourself,
This long-lost, long-sought freedom makes you rave.

MARY.
Yonder's a fisher returning to his home;
Poor though it be, would he lend me his wherry,
Quick to congenial shores would I ferry.
Spare is his trade, and labor's his doom;
Rich would I freight his vessel with treasure;

Such a draught should be his as he never had seen;
Wealth should he find in his nets without measure,
Would he but rescue a poor captive queen.

KENNEDY.
Fond, fruitless wishes! See you not from far
How we are followed by observing spies?
A dismal, barbarous prohibition scares
Each sympathetic being from our path.

MARY.
No, gentle Hannah! Trust me, not in vain
My prison gates are opened. This small grace
Is harbinger of greater happiness.
No! I mistake not; 'tis the active hand
Of love to which I owe this kind indulgence.
I recognize in this the mighty arm
Of Leicester. They will by degrees expand
My prison; will accustom me, through small,
To greater liberty, until at last
I shall behold the face of him whose hand
Will dash my fetters off, and that forever.

KENNEDY.
Oh, my dear queen! I cannot reconcile
These contradictions. 'Twas but yesterday
That they announced your death, and all at once,
To-day, you have such liberty. Their chains
Are also loosed, as I have oft been told,
Whom everlasting liberty awaits.

   [Hunting horns at a distance.

MARY.
Hear'st then the bugle, so blithely resounding?
Hear'st thou its echoes through wood and through plain?
Oh, might I now, on my nimble steed bounding,
Join with the jocund, the frolicsome train.

[Hunting horns again heard.

Again! Oh, this sad and this pleasing remembrance!
These are the sounds which, so sprightly and clear,
Oft, when with music the hounds and the horn
So cheerfully welcomed the break of the morn,
On the heaths of the Highlands delighted my ear.

SCENE II.

   Enter PAULET.

PAULET.
Well, have I acted right at last, my lady?
Do I for once, at least, deserve your thanks?

MARY.
How! Do I owe this favor, sir, to you?

PAULET.
Why not to me? I visited the court,
And gave the queen your letter.

MARY.
        Did you give it?

In very truth did you deliver it?
And is this freedom which I now enjoy
The happy consequence?

PAULET (significantly).
     Nor that alone;
Prepare yourself to see a greater still.

MARY.
A greater still! What do you mean by that?

PAULET.
You heard the bugle-horns?

MARY (starting back with foreboding apprehension).
     You frighten me.

PAULET.
The queen is hunting in the neighborhood----

MARY.
     What!

PAULET.
In a few moments she'll appear before you.

KENNEDY (hastening towards MARY, and about to fall).
How fare you, dearest lady? You grow pale.

PAULET.
How? Is't not well? Was it not then your prayer?
'Tis granted now, before it was expected;
You who had ever such a ready speech,

Now summon all your powers of eloquence,
The important time to use them now is come.

MARY.
Oh, why was I not told of this before?
Now I am not prepared for it--not now
What, as the greatest favor, I besought,
Seems to me now most fearful; Hannah, come,
Lead me into the house, till I collect
My spirits.

PAULET.
    Stay; you must await her here.
Yes! I believe you may be well alarmed
To stand before your judge.

SCENE III.

Enter the EARL OF SHREWSBURY.

MARY.
    'Tis not for that, O God!
Far other thoughts possess me now.
Oh, worthy Shrewsbury! You come as though
You were an angel sent to me from heaven.
I cannot, will not see her. Save me, save me
From the detested sight!

SHREWSBURY.
    Your majesty,
Command yourself, and summon all your courage,

'Tis the decisive moment of your fate.

MARY.
For years I've waited, and prepared myself.
For this I've studied, weighed, and written down
Each word within the tablet of my memory
That was to touch and move her to compassion.
Forgotten suddenly, effaced is all,
And nothing lives within me at this moment
But the fierce, burning feeling of my wrongs.
My heart is turned to direst hate against her;
All gentle thoughts, all sweet forgiving words,
Are gone, and round me stand with grisly mien,
The fiends of hell, and shake their snaky locks!

SHREWSBURY.
Command your wild, rebellious blood;--constrain
The bitterness which fills your heart. No good
Ensues when hatred is opposed to hate.
How much soe'er the inward struggle cost
You must submit to stern necessity,
The power is in her hand, be therefore humble.

MARY.
To her? I never can.

SHREWSBURY.
    But pray, submit.
Speak with respect, with calmness! Strive to move
Her magnanimity; insist not now
Upon your rights, not now--'tis not the season.

MARY.

Ah! woe is me! I've prayed for my destruction,
And, as a curse to me, my prayer is heard.
We never should have seen each other--never!
Oh, this can never, never come to good.
Rather in love could fire and water meet,
The timid lamb embrace the roaring tiger!
I have been hurt too grievously; she hath
Too grievously oppressed me;--no atonement
Can make us friends!

SHREWSBURY.
    First see her, face to face:
Did I not see how she was moved at reading
Your letter? How her eyes were drowned in tears?
No--she is not unfeeling; only place
More confidence in her. It was for this
That I came on before her, to entreat you
To be collected--to admonish you----

MARY (seizing his hand).
Oh, Talbot! you have ever been my friend,
Had I but stayed beneath your kindly care!
They have, indeed, misused me, Shrewsbury.

SHREWSBURY.
Let all be now forgot, and only think
How to receive her with submissiveness.

MARY.
Is Burleigh with her, too, my evil genius?

SHREWSBURY.
No one attends her but the Earl of Leicester.

MARY.
Lord Leicester?

SHREWSBURY.
    Fear not him; it is not he
Who wishes your destruction;--'twas his work
That here the queen hath granted you this meeting.

MARY.
Ah! well I knew it.

SHREWSBURY.
    What?

PAULET.
    The queen approaches.

[They all draw aside; MARY alone remains, leaning on KENNEDY.

SCENE IV.

The same, ELIZABETH, EARL OF LEICESTER, and Retinue.

ELIZABETH (to LEICESTER).
What seat is that, my lord?

LEICESTER.
    'Tis Fotheringay.

ELIZABETH (to SHREWSBURY).

My lord, send back our retinue to London;
The people crowd too eager in the roads,
We'll seek a refuge in this quiet park.

   [TALBOT sends the train away. She looks steadfastly at MARY,
    as she speaks further with PAULET.

My honest people love me overmuch.
These signs of joy are quite idolatrous.
Thus should a God be honored, not a mortal.

MARY (who the whole time had leaned, almost fainting, on KENNEDY, rises
  now, and her eyes meet the steady, piercing look of ELIZABETH; she
  shudders and throws herself again upon KENNEDY'S bosom).
O God! from out these features speaks no heart.

ELIZABETH.
What lady's that?

  [A general, embarrassed silence.

LEICESTER.
    You are at Fotheringay,
My liege!

ELIZABETH (as if surprised, casting an angry look at LEICESTER).
Who hath done this, my Lord of Leicester?

LEICESTER.
'Tis past, my queen;--and now that heaven hath led
Your footsteps hither, be magnanimous;
And let sweet pity be triumphant now.

SHREWSBURY.
Oh, royal mistress! yield to our entreaties;
Oh, cast your eyes on this unhappy one
Who stands dissolved in anguish.

   [MARY collects herself, and begins to advance towards
   ELIZABETH, stops shuddering at half way: her action
   expresses the most violent internal struggle.

ELIZABETH.
         How, my lords!
Which of you then announced to me a prisoner
Bowed down by woe? I see a haughty one
By no means humbled by calamity.

MARY.
Well, be it so:--to this will I submit.
Farewell high thought, and pride of noble mind!
I will forget my dignity, and all
My sufferings; I will fall before her feet
Who hath reduced me to this wretchedness.

   [She turns towards the QUEEN.

The voice of heaven decides for you, my sister.
Your happy brows are now with triumph crowned,
I bless the Power Divine which thus hath raised you.
But in your turn be merciful, my sister;
         [She kneels.
Let me not lie before you thus disgraced;
Stretch forth your hand, your royal hand, to raise
Your sister from the depths of her distress.

ELIZABETH (stepping back).
You are where it becomes you, Lady Stuart;
And thankfully I prize my God's protection,
Who hath not suffered me to kneel a suppliant
Thus at your feet, as you now kneel at mine.

MARY (with increasing energy of feeling).
Think on all earthly things, vicissitudes.
Oh! there are gods who punish haughty pride:
Respect them, honor them, the dreadful ones
Who thus before thy feet have humbled me!
Before these strangers' eyes dishonor not
Yourself in me: profane not, nor disgrace
The royal blood of Tudor. In my veins
It flows as pure a stream as in your own.
Oh, for God's pity, stand not so estranged
And inaccessible, like some tall cliff,
Which the poor shipwrecked mariner in vain
Struggles to seize, and labors to embrace.
My all, my life, my fortune now depends
Upon the influence of my words and tears;
That I may touch your heart, oh, set mine free.
If you regard me with those icy looks
My shuddering heart contracts itself, the stream
Of tears is dried, and frigid horror chains
The words of supplication in my bosom!

ELIZABETH (cold and severe).
What would you say to me, my Lady Stuart?
You wished to speak with me; and I, forgetting
The queen, and all the wrongs I have sustained,
Fulfil the pious duty of the sister,

And grant the boon you wished for of my presence.
Yet I, in yielding to the generous feelings
Of magnanimity, expose myself
To rightful censure, that I stoop so low.
For well you know you would have had me murdered.

MARY.
Oh! how shall I begin? Oh, how shall I
So artfully arrange my cautious words
That they may touch, yet not offend your heart?
Strengthen my words, O Heaven! and take from them
Whate'er might wound. Alas! I cannot speak
In my own cause without impeaching you,
And that most heavily, I wish not so;
You have not as you ought behaved to me:
I am a queen, like you: yet you have held me
Confined in prison. As a suppliant
I came to you, yet you in me insulted
The pious use of hospitality;
Slighting in me the holy law of nations,
Immured me in a dungeon--tore from me
My friends and servants; to unseemly want
I was exposed, and hurried to the bar
Of a disgraceful, insolent tribunal.
No more of this;--in everlasting silence
Be buried all the cruelties I suffered!
See--I will throw the blame of all on fate,
'Twere not your fault, no more than it was mine.
An evil spirit rose from the abyss,
To kindle in our hearts the flame of hate,
By which our tender youth had been divided.
It grew with us, and bad, designing men
Fanned with their ready breath the fatal fire:

Frantics, enthusiasts, with sword and dagger
Armed the uncalled-for hand! This is the curse
Of kings, that they, divided, tear the world
In pieces with their hatred, and let loose
The raging furies of all hellish strife!
No foreign tongue is now between us, sister,

[Approaching her confidently, and with a flattering tone.

Now stand we face to face; now, sister, speak:
Name but my crime, I'll fully satisfy you,--
Alas! had you vouchsafed to hear me then,
When I so earnest sought to meet your eye,
It never would have come to this, nor would,
Here in this mournful place, have happened now
This so distressful, this so mournful meeting.

ELIZABETH.
My better stars preserved me. I was warned,
And laid not to my breast the poisonous adder!
Accuse not fate! your own deceitful heart
It was, the wild ambition of your house
As yet no enmities had passed between us,
When your imperious uncle, the proud priest,
Whose shameless hand grasps at all crowns, attacked me
With unprovoked hostility, and taught
You, but too docile, to assume my arms,
To vest yourself with my imperial title,
And meet me in the lists in mortal strife:
What arms employed he not to storm my throne?
The curses of the priests, the people's sword,
The dreadful weapons of religious frenzy;--
Even here in my own kingdom's peaceful haunts

He fanned the flames of civil insurrection;
But God is with me, and the haughty priest
Has not maintained the field. The blow was aimed
Full at my head, but yours it is which falls!

MARY.
I'm in the hand of heaven. You never will
Exert so cruelly the power it gives you.

ELIZABETH.
Who shall prevent me? Say, did not your uncle
Set all the kings of Europe the example,
How to conclude a peace with those they hate.
Be mine the school of Saint Bartholomew;
What's kindred then to me, or nation's laws?
The church can break the bands of every duty;
It consecrates the regicide, the traitor;
I only practise what your priests have taught!
Say then, what surety can be offered me,
Should I magnanimously loose your bonds?
Say, with what lock can I secure your faith,
Which by Saint Peter's keys cannot be opened?
Force is my only surety; no alliance
Can be concluded with a race of vipers.

MARY.
Oh! this is but your wretched, dark suspicion!
For you have constantly regarded me
But as a stranger, and an enemy.
Had you declared me heir to your dominions,
As is my right, then gratitude and love
In me had fixed, for you, a faithful friend
And kinswoman.

ELIZABETH.
>   Your friendship is abroad,
Your house is papacy, the monk your brother.
Name you my successor! The treacherous snare!
That in my life you might seduce my people;
And, like a sly Armida, in your net
Entangle all our noble English youth;
That all might turn to the new rising sun,
And I----

MARY.
O sister, rule your realm in peace;
I give up every claim to these domains--
Alas! the pinions of my soul are lamed;
Greatness entices me no more: your point
Is gained; I am but Mary's shadow now--
My noble spirit is at last broke down
By long captivity:--you've done your worst
On me; you have destroyed me in my bloom!
Now, end your work, my sister;--speak at length
The word, which to pronounce has brought you hither;
For I will ne'er believe that you are come,
To mock unfeelingly your hapless victim.
Pronounce this word;--say, "Mary, you are free:
You have already felt my power,--learn now
To honor too my generosity."
Say this, and I will take my life, will take
My freedom, as a present from your hands.
One word makes all undone;--I wait for it;--
Oh, let it not be needlessly delayed.
Woe to you if you end not with this word!
For should you not, like some divinity,

Dispensing noble blessings, quit me now,
Then, sister, not for all this island's wealth,
For all the realms encircled by the deep,
Would I exchange my present lot for yours.

ELIZABETH.
And you confess at last that you are conquered:
Are all your schemes run out? No more assassins
Now on the road? Will no adventurer
Attempt again for you the sad achievement?
Yes, madam, it is over:--you'll seduce
No mortal more. The world has other cares;--
None is ambitious of the dangerous honor
Of being your fourth husband--you destroy
Your wooers like your husbands.

MARY (starting angrily).
        Sister, sister!--
Grant me forbearance, all ye powers of heaven!

ELIZABETH (regards her long with a look of proud contempt).
Those then, my Lord of Leicester, are the charms
Which no man with impunity can view,
Near which no woman dare to stand?
In sooth, this honor has been cheaply gained;
She who to all is common, may with ease
Become the common object of applause.

MARY.
This is too much!

ELIZABETH (laughing insultingly).
      You show us now, indeed,

Your real face; till now 'twas but the mask.

MARY (burning with rage, yet dignified and noble).
My sins were human, and the faults of youth:
Superior force misled me. I have never
Denied or sought to hide it: I despised
All false appearance, as became a queen.
The worst of me is known, and I can say,
That I am better than the fame I bear.
Woe to you! when, in time to come, the world
Shall draw the robe of honor from your deeds,
With which thy arch-hypocrisy has veiled
The raging flames of lawless, secret lust.
Virtue was not your portion from your mother;
Well know we what it was which brought the head
Of Anna Boleyn to the fatal block.

SHREWSBURY (stepping between both QUEENS).
Oh! Heaven! Alas, and must it come to this!
Is this the moderation, the submission,
My lady?----

MARY.
    Moderation! I've supported
What human nature can support: farewell,
Lamb-hearted resignation, passive patience,
Fly to thy native heaven; burst at length
Thy bonds, come forward from thy dreary cave,
In all thy fury, long suppressed rancor!
And thou, who to the angered basilisk
Impart'st the murderous glance, oh, arm my tongue
With poisoned darts!

SHREWSBURY.
>She is beside herself!
Exasperated, mad! My liege, forgive her.

[ELIZABETH, speechless with anger, casts enraged looks at MARY.

LEICESTER (in the most violent agitation; he seeks to lead ELIZABETH away).
Attend not to her rage! Away, away,
From this disastrous place!

MARY (raising her voice).
>A bastard soils,
Profanes the English throne! The generous Britons
Are cheated by a juggler, [whose whole figure
Is false and painted, heart as well as face!]
If right prevailed, you now would in the dust
Before me lie, for I'm your rightful monarch!

[ELIZABETH hastily quits the stage; the lords follow her in the greatest consternation.

SCENE V.

MARY, KENNEDY.

KENNEDY.
What have you done? She has gone hence in wrath
All hope is over now!

MARY (still quite beside herself).

Gone hence in wrath!
She carries death within her heart! I know it.

[Falling on KENNEDY'S bosom.

Now I am happy, Hannah! and at last,
After whole years of sorrow and abasement,
One moment of victorious revenge
A weight falls off my heart, a weight of mountains;
I plunged the steel in my oppressor's breast!

KENNEDY.
Unhappy lady! Frenzy overcomes you.
Yes, you have wounded your inveterate foe;
'Tis she who wields the lightning, she is queen,
You have insulted her before her minion.

MARY.
I have abased her before Leicester's eyes;
He saw it, he was witness of my triumph.
How did I hurl her from her haughty height,
He saw it, and his presence strengthened me.

SCENE VI.

Enter MORTIMER.

KENNEDY.
Oh, Sir! What an occurrence!

MORTIMER.

I heard all--

[Gives the nurse a sign to repair to her post,
and draws nearer; his whole appearance expresses
the utmost violence of passion.

Thine is the palm;--thou trod'st her to the dust!--
Thou wast the queen, she was the malefactor;--
I am transported with thy noble courage;--
Yes! I adore thee; like a Deity,
My sense is dazzled by thy heavenly beams.

MARY (with vivacity and expectation).
You spoke with Leicester, gave my letter to him.
My present, too?--oh, speak, sir.

MORTIMER (beholding her with glowing looks).
           How thy noble,
Thy royal indignation shone, and cast
A glory round thy beauty; yes, by heavens,
Thou art the fairest woman upon earth!

MARY.
Sir, satisfy, I beg you, my impatience;
What says his lordship? Say, sir, may I hope?

MORTIMER.
Who?--he?--he is a wretch, a very coward,
Hope naught from him; despise him, and forget him!

MARY.
What say you?

MORTIMER.
>He deliver, and possess you!
Why let him dare it:--he!--he must with me
In mortal contest first deserve the prize!

MARY.
You gave him not my letter? Then, indeed
My hopes are lost!

MORTIMER.
>The coward loves his life.
Whoe'er would rescue you, and call you his,
Must boldly dare affront e'en death itself!

MARY.
Will he do nothing for me?

MORTIMER.
>Speak not of him.
What can he do? What need have we of him?
I will release you; I alone.

MARY.
>Alas!
What power have you?

MORTIMER.
>Deceive yourself no more;
Think not your case is now as formerly;
The moment that the queen thus quitted you,
And that your interview had ta'en this turn,
All hope was lost, each way of mercy shut.
Now deeds must speak, now boldness must decide,

To compass all must all be hazarded;
You must be free before the morning break.

MARY.
What say you, sir--to-night?--impossible!

MORTIMER.
Hear what has been resolved:--I led my friends
Into a private chapel, where a priest
Heard our confession, and, for every sin
We had committed, gave us absolution;
He gave us absolution too, beforehand,
For every crime we might commit in future;
He gave us too the final sacrament,
And we are ready for the final journey.

MARY.
Oh, what an awful, dreadful preparation!

MORTIMER.
We scale, this very night, the castle's walls;
The keys are in my power; the guards we murder!
Then from thy chamber bear thee forcibly.
Each living soul must die beneath our hands,
That none remain who might disclose the deed.

MARY.
And Drury, Paulet, my two keepers, they
Would sooner spill their dearest drop of blood.

MORTIMER.
They fall the very first beneath my steel.

MARY.
What, sir! Your uncle? How! Your second father!

MORTIMER.
Must perish by my hand--I murder him!

MARY.
Oh, bloody outrage!

MORTIMER.
    We have been absolved
Beforehand; I may perpetrate the worst;
I can, I will do so!

MARY.
    Oh, dreadful, dreadful!

MORTIMER.
And should I be obliged to kill the queen,
I've sworn upon the host, it must be done!

MARY.
No, Mortimer; ere so much blood for me----

MORTIMER.
What is the life of all compared to thee,
And to my love? The bond which holds the world
Together may be loosed, a second deluge
Come rolling on, and swallow all creation!
Henceforth I value nothing; ere I quit
My hold on thee, may earth and time be ended!

MARY (retiring)

Heavens! Sir, what language, and what looks! They scare,
They frighten me!

MORTIMER (with unsteady looks, expressive of great madness).
     Life's but a moment--death
Is but a moment too. Why! let them drag me
To Tyburn, let them tear me limb from limb,
With red-hot pincers----
  [Violently approaching her with extended arms.
     If I clasp but thee
Within my arms, thou fervently beloved!

MARY.
Madman, avaunt!

MORTIMER.
     To rest upon this bosom,
To press upon this passion-breathing mouth----

MARY.
Leave me, for God's sake, sir; let me go in----

MORTIMER.
He is a madman who neglects to clasp
His bliss in folds that never may be loosed,
When Heaven has kindly given it to his arms.
I will deliver you, and though it cost
A thousand lives, I do it; but I swear,
As God's in Heaven I will possess you too!

MARY.
Oh! will no God, no angel shelter me?
Dread destiny! thou throwest me, in thy wrath,

From one tremendous terror to the other!
Was I then born to waken naught but frenzy?
Do hate and love conspire alike to fright me!

MORTIMER.
Yes, glowing as their hatred is my love;
They would behead thee, they would wound this neck,
So dazzling white, with the disgraceful axe!
Oh! offer to the living god of joy
What thou must sacrifice to bloody hate!
Inspire thy happy lover with those charms
Which are no more thine own. Those golden locks
Are forfeit to the dismal powers of death,
Oh! use them to entwine thy slave forever!

MARY.
Alas! alas! what language must I hear!
My woe, my sufferings should be sacred to you,
Although my royal brows are so no more.

MORTIMER.
The crown is fallen from thy brows, thou hast
No more of earthly majesty. Make trial,
Raise thy imperial voice, see if a friend,
If a deliverer will rise to save you.
Thy moving form alone remains, the high,
The godlike influence of thy heavenly beauty;
This bids me venture all, this arms my hand
With might, and drives me tow'rd the headsman's axe.

MARY.
Oh! who will save me from his raging madness?

MORTIMER.
Service that's bold demands a bold reward.
Why shed their blood the daring? Is not life
Life's highest good? And he a madman who
Casts life away? First will I take my rest,
Upon the breast that glows with love's own fire!

[He presses her violently to his bosom.

MARY.
Oh, must I call for help against the man
Who would deliver me!

MORTIMER.
    Thou'rt not unfeeling,
The world ne'er censured thee for frigid rigor;
The fervent prayer of love can touch thy heart.
Thou mad'st the minstrel Rizzio blest, and gavest
Thyself a willing prey to Bothwell's arms.

MARY.
Presumptuous man!

MORTIMER.
    He was indeed thy tyrant,
Thou trembled'st at his rudeness, whilst thou loved'st him;
Well, then--if only terror can obtain thee--
By the infernal gods!

MARY.
    Away--you're mad!

MORTIMER.

I'll teach thee then before me, too, to tremble.

KENNEDY (entering suddenly).
They're coming--they approach--the park is filled
With men in arms.

MORTIMER (starting and catching at his sword).
    I will defend you-I----

MARY.
O Hannah! save me, save me from his hands.
Where shall I find, poor sufferer, an asylum?
Oh! to what saint shall I address my prayers?
Here force assails me, and within is murder!

  [She flies towards the house, KENNEDY follows her.

SCENE VII.

  MORTIMER, PAULET, and DRURY rush in in the greatest consternation. Attendants hasten over the stage.

PAULET.
Shut all the portals--draw the bridges up.

MORTIMER.
What is the matter, uncle?

PAULET.
    Where is the murderess?

Down with her, down into the darkest dungeon!

MORTIMER.
What is the matter? What has passed?

PAULET.
   The queen!
Accursed hand! Infernal machination!

MORTIMER.
The queen! What queen?

PAULET.
   What queen! The Queen of England;
She has been murdered on the road to London.

 [Hastens into the house.

SCENE VIII.

 MORTIMER, soon after O'KELLY.

MORTIMER (after a pause).
Am I then mad? Came not one running by
But now, and cried aloud, the queen is murdered!
No, no! I did but dream. A feverish fancy
Paints that upon my mind as true and real,
Which but existed in my frantic thoughts.
Who's there? It is O'Kelly. So dismayed!

O'KELLY (rushing in).

Flee, Mortimer, oh! flee--for all is lost!

MORTIMER.
What then is lost?

O'KELLY.
    Stand not on question. Think
On speedy flight.

MORTIMER.
    What has occurred?

O'KELLY.
        Sauvage,
That madman, struck the blow.

MORTIMER.
    It is then true!

O'KELLY.
True, true--oh! save yourself.

MORTIMER (exultingly).
    The queen is murdered--
And Mary shall ascend the English throne!

O'KELLY.
Is murdered! Who said that?

MORTIMER.
    Yourself.

O'KELLY.

She lives,
And I, and you, and all of us are lost.

MORTIMER.
She lives!

O'KELLY.
   The blow was badly aimed, her cloak
Received it. Shrewsbury disarmed the murderer.

MORTIMER.
She lives!

O'KELLY.
   She lives to whelm us all in ruin;
Come, they surround the park already; come.

MORTIMER.
Who did this frantic deed?

O'KELLY.
          It was the monk
From Toulon, whom you saw immersed in thought,
As in the chapel the pope's bull was read,
Which poured anathemas upon the queen.
He wished to take the nearest, shortest way,
To free, with one bold stroke, the church of God,
And gain the crown of martyrdom: he trusted
His purpose only to the priest, and struck
The fatal blow upon the road to London.

MORTIMER (after a long silence).
Alas! a fierce, destructive fate pursues thee,

Unhappy one! Yes--now thy death is fixed;
Thy very angel has prepared thy fall!

O'KELLY.
Say, whither will you take your flight? I go
To hide me in the forests of the north.

MORTIMER.
Fly thither, and may God attend your flight;
I will remain, and still attempt to save
My love; if not, my bed shall be upon her grave.

    [Exeunt at different sides.

ACT IV.

SCENE I.--Antechamber.

   COUNT AUBESPINE, the EARLS Of KENT and LEICESTER.

AUBESPINE.
How fares her majesty? My lords, you see me
Still stunned, and quite beside myself for terror!
How happened it? How was it possible
That in the midst of this most loyal people----

LEICESTER.
The deed was not attempted by the people.
The assassin was a subject of your king,
A Frenchman.

AUBESPINE.
    Sure a lunatic.

LEICESTER.
        A papist,
Count Aubespine!

SCENE II.

Enter BURLEIGH, in conversation with DAVISON.

BURLEIGH.
    Sir; let the death-warrant
Be instantly made out, and pass the seal;
Then let it be presented to the queen;
Her majesty must sign it. Hasten, sir,
We have no time to lose.

DAVISON.
    It shall be done.

    [Exit.

AUBESPINE.
My lord high-treasurer, my faithful heart
Shares in the just rejoicings of the realm.
Praised be almighty Heaven, who hath averted
Assassination from our much-loved queen!

BURLEIGH.
Praised be His name, who thus hath turned to scorn
The malice of our foes!

AUBESPINE.
    May heaven confound
The perpetrator of this cursed deed!

BURLEIGH.
Its perpetrator and its base contriver!

AUBESPINE.
Please you, my lord, to bring me to the queen,

That I may lay the warm congratulations
Of my imperial master at her feet.

BURLEIGH.
There is no need of this.

AUBESPINE (officiously).
  My Lord of Burleigh,
I know my duty.

BURLEIGH.
  Sir, your duty is
To quit, and that without delay, this kingdom.

AUBESPINE (stepping back with surprise).
What! How is this?

BURLEIGH.
  The sacred character
Of an ambassador to-day protects you,
But not to-morrow.

AUBESPINE.
  What's my crime?

BURLEIGH.
  Should I
Once name it, there were then no pardon for it.

AUBESPINE.
I hope, my lord, my charge's privilege----

BURLEIGH.

Screens not a traitor.

LEICESTER and KENT.
    Traitor! How?

AUBESPINE.
          My Lord,
Consider well----

BURLEIGH.
    Your passport was discovered
In the assassin's pocket.

KENT.
        Righteous heaven!

AUBESPINE.
Sir, many passports are subscribed by me;
I cannot know the secret thoughts of men.

BURLEIGH.
He in your house confessed, and was absolved.

AUBESPINE.
My house is open----

BURLEIGH.
    To our enemies.

AUBESPINE.
I claim a strict inquiry.

BURLEIGH.

Tremble at it.

AUBESPINE.
My monarch in my person is insulted,
He will annul the marriage contract.

BURLEIGH.
      That
My royal mistress has annulled already;
England will not unite herself with France.
My Lord of Kent, I give to you the charge
To see Count Aubespine embarked in safety.
The furious populace has stormed his palace,
Where a whole arsenal of arms was found;
Should he be found, they'll tear him limb from limb,
Conceal him till the fury is abated--
You answer for his life.

AUBESPINE.
     I go--I leave
This kingdom where they sport with public treaties
And trample on the laws of nations. Yet
My monarch, be assured, will vent his rage
In direst vengeance!

BURLEIGH.
    Let him seek it here.

[Exeunt KENT and AUBESPINE.

SCENE III.

LEICESTER, BURLEIGH.

LEICESTER.
And thus you loose yourself the knot of union
Which you officiously, uncalled for, bound!
You have deserved but little of your country,
My lord; this trouble was superfluous.

BURLEIGH.
My aim was good, though fate declared against it;
Happy is he who has so fair a conscience!

LEICESTER.
Well know we the mysterious mien of Burleigh
When he is on the hunt for deeds of treason.
Now you are in your element, my lord;
A monstrous outrage has been just committed,
And darkness veils as yet its perpetrators:
Now will a court of inquisition rise;
Each word, each look be weighed; men's very thoughts
Be summoned to the bar. You are, my lord,
The mighty man, the Atlas of the state,
All England's weight lies upon your shoulders.

BURLEIGH.
In you, my lord, I recognize my master;
For such a victory as your eloquence
Has gained I cannot boast.

LEICESTER.
    What means your lordship?

BURLEIGH.
You were the man who knew, behind my back,
To lure the queen to Fotheringay Castle.

LEICESTER.
Behind your back! When did I fear to act
Before your face?

BURLEIGH.
    You led her majesty?
Oh, no--you led her not--it was the queen
Who was so gracious as to lead you thither.

LEICESTER.
What mean you, my lord, by that?

BURLEIGH.
      The noble part
You forced the queen to play! The glorious triumph
Which you prepared for her! Too gracious princess!
So shamelessly, so wantonly to mock
Thy unsuspecting goodness, to betray thee
So pitiless to thy exulting foe!
This, then, is the magnanimity, the grace
Which suddenly possessed you in the council!
The Stuart is for this so despicable,
So weak an enemy, that it would scarce
Be worth the pains to stain us with her blood.
A specious plan! and sharply pointed too;
'Tis only pity this sharp point is broken.

LEICESTER.
Unworthy wretch! this instant follow me,

And answer at the throne this insolence.

BURLEIGH.
You'll find me there, my lord; and look you well
That there your eloquence desert you not.

   [Exit.

SCENE IV.

   LEICESTER alone, then MORTIMER.

LEICESTER.
I am detected! All my plot's disclosed!
How has my evil genius tracked my steps!
Alas! if he has proofs, if she should learn
That I have held a secret correspondence
With her worst enemy; how criminal
Shall I appear to her! How false will then
My counsel seem, and all the fatal pains
I took to lure the queen to Fotheringay!
I've shamefully betrayed, I have exposed her
To her detested enemy's revilings!
Oh! never, never can she pardon that.
All will appear as if premeditated.
The bitter turn of this sad interview,
The triumph and the tauntings of her rival;
Yes, e'en the murderous hand which had prepared
A bloody, monstrous, unexpected fate;
All, all will be ascribed to my suggestions!
I see no rescue! nowhere--ha! Who comes?

[MORTIMER enters in the most violent uneasiness, and looks with apprehension round him.

MORTIMER.
Lord Leicester! Is it you! Are we alone?

LEICESTER.
Ill-fated wretch, away! What seek you here?

MORTIMER.
They are upon our track--upon yours, too;
Be vigilant!

LEICESTER.
    Away, away!

MORTIMER.
        They know
That private conferences have been held
At Aubespine's----

LEICESTER.
      What's that to me?

MORTIMER.
          They know, too,
That the assassin----

LEICESTER.
     That is your affair--
Audacious wretch! to dare to mix my name
In your detested outrage: go; defend

Your bloody deeds yourself!

MORTIMER.
    But only hear me.

LEICESTER (violently enraged).
Down, down to hell! Why cling you at my heels
Like an infernal spirit! I disclaim you;
I know you not; I make no common cause
With murderers!

MORTIMER.
    You will not hear me, then!
I came to warn you; you too are detected.

LEICESTER.
How! What?

MORTIMER.
    Lord Burleigh went to Fotheringay
Just as the luckless deed had been attempted;
Searched with strict scrutiny the queen's apartments,
And found there----

LEICESTER.
    What?

MORTIMER.
    A letter which the queen
Had just addressed to you----

LEICESTER.
    Unhappy woman!

MORTIMER.
In which she calls on you to keep your word,
Renews the promise of her hand, and mentions
The picture which she sent you.

LEICESTER.
      Death and hell!

MORTIMER.
Lord Burleigh has the letter.

LEICESTER.
      I am lost!

  [During the following speech of MORTIMER, LEICESTER
  goes up and down as in despair.

MORTIMER.
Improve the moment; be beforehand with him,
And save yourself--save her! An oath can clear
Your fame; contrive excuses to avert
The worst. I am disarmed, can do no more;
My comrades are dispersed--to pieces fallen
Our whole confederacy. For Scotland I
To rally such new friends as there I may.
'Tis now your turn, my lord; try what your weight,
What bold assurance can effect.

LEICESTER (stops suddenly as if resolved).
      I will.

  [Goes to the door, opens it, and calls.

Who waits without? Guards! seize this wretched traitor!

  [To the officer, who comes in with soldiers.

And guard him closely! A most dreadful plot
Is brought to light--I'll to her majesty.

MORTIMER (stands for a time petrified with wonder; collects himself soon, and follows LEICESTER with his looks expressive of the most sovereign contempt).
Infamous wretch! But I deserve it all.
Who told me then to trust this practised villain?
Now o'er my head he strides, and on my fall
He builds the bridge of safety! be it so;
Go, save thyself--my lips are sealed forever;
I will not join even thee in my destruction;
I would not own thee, no, not even in death;
Life is the faithless villain's only good!

  [To the officer of the guard, who steps forward to seize him.

What wilt thou, slave of tyranny, with me?
I laugh to scorn thy threatenings; I am free.

  [Drawing a dagger.

OFFICER.
He's armed; rush in and wrest his weapon from him.

  [They rush upon him, he defends himself.

MORTIMER (raising his voice).

And in this latest moment shall my heart
Expand itself in freedom, and my tongue
Shall break this long constraint. Curse and destruction
Light on you all who have betrayed your faith,
Your God, and your true sovereign! Who, alike
To earthly Mary false as to the heavenly,
Have sold your duties to this bastard queen!

OFFICER.
Hear you these blasphemies? Rush forward--seize him.

MORTIMER.
Beloved queen! I could not set thee free;
Yet take a lesson from me how to die.
Mary, thou holy one, O! pray for me!
And take me to thy heavenly home on high.

[Stabs himself, and falls into the arms of the guard.

SCENE V.

The apartment of the Queen.

ELIZABETH, with a letter in her hand, BURLEIGH.

ELIZABETH.
To lure me thither! trifle with me thus!
The traitor! Thus to lead me, as in triumph,
Into the presence of his paramour!
Oh, Burleigh! ne'er was woman so deceived.

BURLEIGH.
I cannot yet conceive what potent means,
What magic he exerted, to surprise
My queen's accustomed prudence.

ELIZABETH.
      Oh, I die
For shame! How must he laugh to scorn my weakness!
I thought to humble her, and was myself
The object of her bitter scorn.

BURLEIGH.
      By this
You see how faithfully I counselled you.

ELIZABETH.
Oh, I am sorely punished, that I turned
My ear from your wise counsels; yet I thought
I might confide in him. Who could suspect
Beneath the vows of faithfullest devotion
A deadly snare? In whom can I confide
When he deceives me? He, whom I have made
The greatest of the great, and ever set
The nearest to my heart, and in this court
Allowed to play the master and the king.

BURLEIGH.
Yet in that very moment he betrayed you,
Betrayed you to this wily Queen of Scots.

ELIZABETH.
Oh, she shall pay me for it with her life!
Is the death-warrant ready?

BURLEIGH.
> 'Tis prepared
As you commanded.

ELIZABETH.
> She shall surely die--
He shall behold her fall, and fall himself!
I've driven him from my heart. No longer love,
Revenge alone is there: and high as once
He stood, so low and shameful be his fall!
A monument of my severity,
As once the proud example of my weakness.
Conduct him to the Tower; let a commission
Of peers be named to try him. He shall feel
In its full weight the rigor of the law.

BURLEIGH.
But he will seek thy presence; he will clear----

ELIZABETH.
How can he clear himself? Does not the letter
Convict him. Oh, his crimes are manifest!

BURLEIGH.
But thou art mild and gracious! His appearance,
His powerful presence----

ELIZABETH.
> I will never see him;
No never, never more. Are orders given
Not to admit him should he come?

BURLEIGH.
>'Tis done.

PAGE (entering).
The Earl of Leicester!

ELIZABETH.
>The presumptuous man!
I will not see him. Tell him that I will not.

PAGE.
I am afraid to bring my lord this message,
Nor would he credit it.

ELIZABETH.
>And I have raised him
So high that my own servants tremble more
At him than me!

BURLEIGH (to the PAGE).
>The queen forbids his presence.

[The PAGE retires slowly.

ELIZABETH (after a pause).
Yet, if it still were possible? If he
Could clear himself? Might it not be a snare
Laid by the cunning one, to sever me
From my best friends--the ever-treacherous harlot!
She might have writ the letter, but to raise
Poisonous suspicion in my heart, to ruin
The man she hates.

BURLEIGH.
>Yet, gracious queen, consider.

SCENE VI.

>LEICESTER (bursts open the door with violence, and enters with an imperious air).

LEICESTER.
Fain would I see the shameless man who dares
Forbid me the apartments of my queen!

ELIZABETH (avoiding his sight).

Audacious slave!

LEICESTER.
>To turn me from the door!

If for a Burleigh she be visible,
She must be so to me!

BURLEIGH.
>My lord, you are
Too bold, without permission to intrude.

LEICESTER.
My lord, you are too arrogant, to take
The lead in these apartments. What! Permission!
I know of none who stands so high at court
As to permit my doings, or refuse them.

[Humbly approaching ELIZABETH.

'Tis from my sovereign's lips alone that I----

ELIZABETH (without looking at him).
Out of my sight, deceitful, worthless traitor!

LEICESTER.
'Tis not my gracious queen I hear, but Burleigh,
My enemy, in these ungentle words.
To my imperial mistress I appeal;
Thou hast lent him thine ear; I ask the like.

ELIZABETH.
Speak, shameless wretch! Increase your crime--deny it.

LEICESTER.
Dismiss this troublesome intruder first.
Withdraw, my lord; it is not of your office
To play the third man here: between the queen
And me there is no need of witnesses.
Retire----

ELIZABETH (to BURLEIGH).
   Remain, my lord; 'tis my command.

LEICESTER.
What has a third to do 'twixt thee and me?
I have to clear myself before my queen,
My worshipped queen; I will maintain the rights
Which thou hast given me; these rights are sacred,

And I insist upon it, that my lord
Retire.

ELIZABETH.
   This haughty tone befits you well.

LEICESTER.
It well befits me; am not I the man,
The happy man, to whom thy gracious favor
Has given the highest station? this exalts me
Above this Burleigh, and above them all.
Thy heart imparted me this rank, and what
Thy favor gave, by heavens I will maintain
At my life's hazard. Let him go, it needs
Two moments only to exculpate me.

ELIZABETH.
Think not, with cunning words, to hide the truth.

LEICESTER.
That fear from him, so voluble of speech:
But what I say is to the heart addressed;
And I will justify what I have dared
To do, confiding in thy generous favor,
Before thy heart alone. I recognize
No other jurisdiction.

ELIZABETH.
    Base deceiver
'Tis this, e'en this, which above all condemns you.
My lord, produce the letter.

  [To BURLEIGH.

BURLEIGH.
>	Here it is.

LEICESTER (running over the letter without losing his presence of mind).
'Tis Mary Stuart's hand----

ELIZABETH.
>	Read and be dumb!

LEICESTER (having read it quietly).
Appearance is against me, yet I hope
I shall not by appearances be judged.

ELIZABETH.
Can you deny your secret correspondence
With Mary?--that she sent and you received
Her picture, that you gave her hopes of rescue?

LEICESTER.
It were an easy matter, if I felt
That I were guilty of a crime, to challenge
The testimony of my enemy:
Yet bold is my good conscience. I confess
That she hath said the truth.

ELIZABETH.
>	Well then, thou wretch!

BURLEIGH.
His own words sentence him----

ELIZABETH.

   Out of my sight!
Away! Conduct the traitor to the Tower!

LEICESTER.
I am no traitor; it was wrong, I own,
To make a secret of this step to thee;
Yet pure was my intention, it was done
To search into her plots and to confound them.

ELIZABETH.
Vain subterfuge!

BURLEIGH.
  And do you think, my lord----

LEICESTER.
I've played a dangerous game, I know it well,
And none but Leicester dare be bold enough
To risk it at this court. The world must know
How I detest this Stuart, and the rank
Which here I hold; my monarch's confidence,
With which she honors me, must sure suffice
To overturn all doubt of my intentions.
Well may the man thy favor above all
Distinguishes pursue a daring course
To do his duty!

BURLEIGH.
  If the course was good,
Wherefore conceal it?

LEICESTER.
  You are used, my lord,

To prate before you act; the very chime
Of your own deeds. This is your manner, lord;
But mine is first to act, and then to speak.

BURLEIGH.
Yes, now you speak because you must.

LEICESTER (measuring him proudly and disdainfully with his eyes).
        And you
Boast of a wonderful, a mighty action,
That you have saved the queen, have snatched away
The mask from treachery; all is known to you;
You think, forsooth, that nothing can escape
Your penetrating eyes. Poor, idle boaster!
In spite of all your cunning, Mary Stuart
Was free to-day, had I not hindered it.

BURLEIGH.
        How? You?

LEICESTER.
Yes, I, my lord; the queen confided
In Mortimer; she opened to the youth
Her inmost soul! Yes, she went further still;
She gave him, too, a secret, bloody charge,
Which Paulet had before refused with horror.
Say, is it so, or not?

  [The QUEEN and BURLEIGH look at one another with astonishment.

BURLEIGH.
        Whence know ye this?

LEICESTER.
Nay, is it not a fact? Now answer me.
And where, my lord, where were your thousand eyes,
Not to discover Mortimer was false?
That he, the Guise's tool, and Mary's creature,
A raging papist, daring fanatic,
Was come to free the Stuart, and to murder
The Queen of England!

ELIZABETH (with the utmost astonishment).
    How! This Mortimer!

LEICESTER.
'Twas he through whom our correspondence passed.
This plot it was which introduced me to him.
This very day she was to have been torn
From her confinement; he, this very moment,
Disclosed his plan to me: I took him prisoner,
And gave him to the guard, when in despair
To see his work o'erturned, himself unmasked,
He slew himself!

ELIZABETH.
    Oh, I indeed have been
Deceived beyond example, Mortimer!

BURLEIGH.
This happened then but now? Since last we parted?

LEICESTER.
For my own sake, I must lament the deed;
That he was thus cut off. His testimony,
Were he alive, had fully cleared my fame,

And freed me from suspicion; 'twas for this
That I surrendered him to open justice.
I thought to choose the most impartial course
To verify and fix my innocence
Before the world.

BURLEIGH.
     He killed himself, you say
Is't so? Or did you kill him?

LEICESTER.
      Vile suspicion!
Hear but the guard who seized him.
  [*He goes to the door, and calls.*
      Ho! who waits?
  [*Enter the officer of the guard.*
Sir, tell the queen how Mortimer expired.

OFFICER.
I was on duty in the palace porch,
When suddenly my lord threw wide the door,
And ordered me to take the knight in charge,
Denouncing him a traitor: upon this
He grew enraged, and with most bitter curses
Against our sovereign and our holy faith,
He drew a dagger, and before the guards
Could hinder his intention, plunged the steel
Into his heart, and fell a lifeless corpse.

LEICESTER.
'Tis well; you may withdraw. Her majesty
Has heard enough.

[The officer withdraws.

ELIZABETH.

    Oh, what a deep abyss
Of monstrous deeds?

LEICESTER.
    Who was it, then, my queen,
Who saved you? Was it Burleigh? Did he know
The dangers which surrounded you? Did he
Avert them from your head? Your faithful Leicester
Was your good angel.

BURLEIGH.
    This same Mortimer
Died most conveniently for you, my lord.

ELIZABETH.
What I should say I know not. I believe you,
And I believe you not. I think you guilty,
And yet I think you not. A curse on her
Who caused me all this anguish.

LEICESTER.
    She must die;
I now myself consent unto her death.
I formerly advised you to suspend
The sentence, till some arm should rise anew
On her behalf; the case has happened now,
And I demand her instant execution.

BURLEIGH.

You give this counsel? You?

LEICESTER.
   Howe'er it wound
My feelings to be forced to this extreme,
Yet now I see most clearly, now I feel
That the queen's welfare asks this bloody victim.
'Tis my proposal, therefore, that the writ
Be drawn at once to fix the execution.

BURLEIGH (to the QUEEN).
Since, then, his lordship shows such earnest zeal,
Such loyalty, 'twere well were he appointed
To see the execution of the sentence.

LEICESTER.
Who? I?

BURLEIGH.
 Yes, you; you surely ne'er could find
A better means to shake off the suspicion
Which rests upon you still, than to command
Her, whom 'tis said you love, to be beheaded.

ELIZABETH (looking steadfastly at LEICESTER).
My lord advises well. So be it, then.

LEICESTER.
It were but fit that my exalted rank
Should free me from so mournful a commission,
Which would indeed, in every sense, become
A Burleigh better than the Earl of Leicester.
The man who stands so near the royal person

Should have no knowledge of such fatal scenes:
But yet to prove my zeal, to satisfy
My queen, I waive my charge's privilege,
And take upon myself this hateful duty.

ELIZABETH.
Lord Burleigh shall partake this duty with you.

[To BURLEIGH.

So be the warrant instantly prepared.

[BURLEIGH withdraws; a tumult heard without.

SCENE VII.

The QUEEN, the EARL OF KENT.

ELIZABETH.
How now, my Lord of Kent? What uproar's this
I hear without?

KENT.
  My queen, it is thy people,
Who, round the palace ranged, impatiently
Demand to see their sovereign.

ELIZABETH.
    What's their wish?

KENT.

A panic terror has already spread
Through London, that thy life has been attempted;
That murderers commissioned from the pope
Beset thee; that the Catholics have sworn
To rescue from her prison Mary Stuart,
And to proclaim her queen. Thy loyal people
Believe it, and are mad; her head alone
Can quiet them; this day must be her last.

ELIZABETH.
How! Will they force me, then?

KENT.
        They are resolved----

SCENE VIII.

  Enter BURLEIGH and DAVISON, with a paper.

ELIZABETH.
Well, Davison?

DAVISON (approaches earnestly).
    Your orders are obeyed,
My queen----

ELIZABETH.
    What orders, sir?

[As she is about to take the paper, she shudders, and starts back.

Oh, God!

BURLEIGH.
    Obey
Thy people's voice; it is the voice of God.

ELIZABETH (irresolute, as if in contest with herself)
Oh, my good lord, who will assure me now
That what I hear is my whole people's voice,
The voice of all the world! Ah! much I fear,
That, if I now should listen to the wish
Of the wild multitude, a different voice
Might soon be heard;--and that the very men,
Who now by force oblige me to this step,
May, when 'tis taken, heavily condemn me!

SCENE IX.

  Enter the EARL OF SHREWSBURY (who enters with great emotion).

SHREWSBURY.
Hold fast, my queen, they wish to hurry thee;

  [Seeing DAVISON with the paper.

Be firm--or is it then decided?--is it
Indeed decided? I behold a paper
Of ominous appearance in his hand;
Let it not at this moment meet thy eyes,
My queen!----

ELIZABETH.
> Good Shrewsbury! I am constrained----

SHREWSBURY.
Who can constrain thee? Thou art Queen of England,
Here must thy majesty assert its rights:
Command those savage voices to be silent,
Who take upon themselves to put constraint
Upon thy royal will, to rule thy judgment.
Fear only, blind conjecture, moves thy people;
Thou art thyself beside thyself; thy wrath
Is grievously provoked: thou art but mortal,
And canst not thus ascend the judgment seat.

BURLEIGH.
Judgment has long been past. It is not now
The time to speak but execute the sentence.

KENT (who upon SHREWSBURY'S entry had retired, comes back).
The tumult gains apace; there are no means
To moderate the people.

ELIZABETH (to SHREWSBURY).
> See, my lord,
How they press on.

SHREWSBURY.
> I only ask a respite;
A single word traced by thy hand decides
The peace, the happiness of all thy life!
Thou hast for years considered, let not then
A moment ruled by passion hurry thee--
But a short respite--recollect thyself!

Wait for a moment of tranquillity.

BURLEIGH (violently).
Wait for it--pause--delay--till flames of fire
Consume the realm; until the fifth attempt
Of murder be successful! God, indeed,
Hath thrice delivered thee; thy late escape
Was marvellous, and to expect again
A miracle would be to tempt thy God!

SHREWSBURY.
That God, whose potent hand hath thrice preserved thee,
Who lent my aged feeble arm its strength
To overcome the madman:--he deserves
Thy confidence. I will not raise the voice
Of justice now, for now is not the time;
Thou canst not hear it in this storm of passion.
Yet listen but to this! Thou tremblest now
Before this living Mary--tremble rather
Before the murdered, the beheaded Mary.
She will arise, and quit her grave, will range
A fiend of discord, an avenging ghost,
Around thy realm, and turn thy people's hearts
From their allegiance. For as yet the Britons
Hate her, because they fear her; but most surely
Will they avenge her when she is no more.
They will no more behold the enemy
Of their belief, they will but see in her
The much-lamented issue of their kings
A sacrifice to jealousy and hate.
Then quickly shalt thou see the sudden change
When thou hast done the bloody deed; then go
Through London, seek thy people, which till now

Around thee swarmed delighted; thou shalt see
Another England, and another people;
For then no more the godlike dignity
Of justice, which subdued thy subjects' hearts,
Will beam around thee. Fear, the dread ally
Of tyranny, will shuddering march before thee,
And make a wilderness in every street--
The last, extremest crime thou hast committed.
What head is safe, if the anointed fall?

ELIZABETH.
Ah! Shrewsbury, you saved my life, you turned
The murderous steel aside; why let you not
The dagger take its course? then all these broils
Would have been ended; then, released from doubt,
And free from blame, I should be now at rest
In my still, peaceful grave. In very sooth
I'm weary of my life, and of my crown.
If Heaven decree that one of us two queens
Must perish, to secure the other's life--
And sure it must be so--why should not I
Be she who yields? My people must decide;
I give them back the sovereignty they gave.
God is my witness that I have not lived
For my own sake, but for my people's welfare.
If they expect from this false, fawning Stuart,
The younger sovereign, more happy days,
I will descend with pleasure from the throne,
Again repair to Woodstock's quiet bowers,
Where once I spent my unambitious youth;
Where far removed from all the vanities
Of earthly power, I found within myself
True majesty. I am not made to rule--

A ruler should be made of sterner stuff:
My heart is soft and tender. I have governed
These many years this kingdom happily,
But then I only needed to make happy:
Now, comes my first important regal duty,
And now I feel how weak a thing I am.

BURLEIGH.
Now by mine honor, when I hear my queen,
My royal liege, speak such unroyal words,
I should betray my office, should betray
My country, were I longer to be silent.
You say you love your people 'bove yourself,
Now prove it. Choose not peace for your own heart,
And leave your kingdom to the storms of discord.
Think on the church. Shall, with this papist queen
The ancient superstition be renewed?
The monk resume his sway, the Roman legate
In pomp march hither; lock our churches up,
Dethrone our monarchs? I demand of you
The souls of all your subjects--as you now
Shall act, they all are saved, or all are lost!
Here is no time for mercy;--to promote
Your people's welfare is your highest duty.
If Shrewsbury has saved your life, then I
Will save both you and England--that is more!

ELIZABETH.
I would be left alone. No consolation,
No counsel can be drawn from human aid
In this conjecture:--I will lay my doubts
Before the Judge of all:--I am resolved
To act as He shall teach. Withdraw, my lords.

[To DAVISON, who lays the paper on the table.

You, sir, remain in waiting--close at hand.

[The lords withdraw, SHREWSBURY alone stands for a few moments before the QUEEN, regards her significantly, then withdraws slowly, and with an expression of the deepest anguish.

SCENE X.

ELIZABETH alone.

Oh! servitude of popularity!
Disgraceful slavery! How weary am I
Of flattering this idol, which my soul
Despises in its inmost depth! Oh! when
Shall I once more be free upon this throne?
I must respect the people's voice, and strive
To win the favor of the multitude,
And please the fancies of a mob, whom naught
But jugglers' tricks delight. O call not him
A king who needs must please the world: 'tis he
Alone, who in his actions does not heed
The fickle approbation of mankind.
Have I then practised justice, all my life
Shunned each despotic deed; have I done this
Only to bind my hands against this first,
This necessary act of violence?
My own example now condemns myself!

Had I but been a tyrant, like my sister,
My predecessor, I could fearless then
Have shed this royal blood:--but am I now
Just by my own free choice? No--I was forced
By stern necessity to use this virtue;
Necessity, which binds e'en monarch's wills.
Surrounded by my foes, my people's love
Alone supports me on my envied throne.
All Europe's powers confederate to destroy me;
The pope's inveterate decree declares me
Accursed and excommunicated. France
Betrays me with a kiss, and Spain prepares
At sea a fierce exterminating war;
Thus stand I, in contention with the world,
A poor defenceless woman: I must seek
To veil the spot in my imperial birth,
By which my father cast disgrace upon me:
In vain with princely virtues would I hide it;
The envious hatred of my enemies
Uncovers it, and places Mary Stuart,
A threatening fiend, before me evermore!

[Walking up and down, with quick and agitated steps.

Oh, no! this fear must end. Her head must fall!
I will have peace. She is the very fury
Of my existence; a tormenting demon,
Which destiny has fastened on my soul.
Wherever I had planted me a comfort,
A flattering hope, my way was ever crossed
By this infernal viper! She has torn
My favorite, and my destined bridegroom from me.
The hated name of every ill I feel

Is Mary Stuart--were but she no more
On earth I should be free as mountain air.

   [Standing still.

With what disdain did she look down on me,
As if her eye should blast me like the lightning!
Poor feeble wretch! I bear far other arms,
Their touch is mortal, and thou art no more.

   [Advancing to the table hastily, and taking the pen.

I am a bastard, am I? Hapless wretch,
I am but so the while thou liv'st and breath'st.
Thy death will make my birth legitimate.
The moment I destroy thee is the doubt
Destroyed which hangs o'er my imperial right.
As soon as England has no other choice,
My mother's honor and my birthright triumphs!

   [She signs with resolution; lets her pen then fall,
   and steps back with an expression of terror. After
   a pause she rings.

SCENE XI.

   ELIZABETH, DAVISON.

ELIZABETH.
Where are their lordships?

DAVISON.
>	They are gone to quell
The tumult of the people. The alarm
Was instantly appeased when they beheld
The Earl of Shrewsbury. That's he! exclaimed
A hundred voices--that's the man--he saved
The queen; hear him--the bravest man in England!
And now began the gallant Talbot, blamed
In gentle words the people's violence,
And used such strong, persuasive eloquence,
That all were pacified, and silently
They slunk away.

ELIZABETH.
>	The fickle multitude!
Which turns with every wind. Unhappy he
Who leans upon this reed! 'Tis well, Sir William;
You may retire again----
>	[As he is going towards the door.
>	And, sir, this paper,
Receive it back; I place it in your hands.

DAVISON (casts a look upon the paper, and starts back).
My gracious queen--thy name! 'tis then decided.

ELIZABETH.
I had but to subscribe it--I have done so--
A paper sure cannot decide--a name
Kills not.

DAVISON.
>	Thy name, my queen, beneath this paper
Is most decisive--kills--'tis like the lightning,

Which blasteth as it flies! This fatal scroll
Commands the sheriff and commissioners
To take departure straight for Fotheringay,
And to the Queen of Scots announce her death,
Which must at dawn be put in execution.
There is no respite, no discretion here.
As soon as I have parted with this writ
Her race is run.

ELIZABETH.
    Yes, sir, the Lord has placed
This weighty business in your feeble hands;
Seek him in prayer to light you with his wisdom;
I go--and leave you, sir, to do your duty.

    [Going.

DAVISON.
No; leave me not, my queen, till I have heard
Your will. The only wisdom that I need
Is, word for word, to follow your commands.
Say, have you placed this warrant in my hands
To see that it be speedily enforced?

ELIZABETH.
That you must do as your own prudence dictates.

DAVISON (interrupting her quickly, and alarmed).
Not mine--oh, God forbid! Obedience is
My only prudence here. No point must now
Be left to be decided by your servant.
A small mistake would here be regicide,
A monstrous crime, from which my soul recoils.

Permit me, in this weighty act, to be
Your passive instrument, without a will:--
Tell me in plain, undoubted terms your pleasure,
What with the bloody mandate I should do.

ELIZABETH.
Its name declares its meaning.

DAVISON.
     Do you, then,
My liege, command its instant execution?

ELIZABETH.
I said not that; I tremble but to think it.

DAVISON.
Shall I retain it, then, 'till further orders?

ELIZABETH.
At your own risk; you answer the event.

DAVISON.
I! gracious heavens! Oh, speak, my queen, your pleasure!

ELIZABETH.
My pleasure is that this unhappy business
Be no more mentioned to me; that at last
I may be freed from it, and that forever.

DAVISON.
It costs you but a word--determine then
What shall I do with this mysterious scroll?

ELIZABETH.
I have declared it, plague me, sir, no longer.

DAVISON.
You have declared it, say you? Oh, my queen,
You have said nothing. Please, my gracious mistress,
But to remember----

ELIZABETH (stamps on the ground).
    Insupportable!

DAVISON.
Oh, be indulgent to me! I have entered
Unwittingly, not many months ago,
Upon this office; I know not the language
Of courts and kings. I ever have been reared
In simple, open wise, a plain blunt man.
Be patient with me; nor deny your servant
A light to lead him clearly to his duty.

  [He approaches her in a supplicating posture,
    she turns her back on him; he stands in despair;
    then speaks with a tone of resolution.

Take, take again this paper--take it back!
Within my hands it is a glowing fire.
Select not me, my queen; select not me
To serve you in this terrible conjecture.

ELIZABETH.
Go, sir;--fulfil the duty of your office.

[Exit.

SCENE XII.

DAVISON, then BURLEIGH.

DAVISON.
She goes! She leaves me doubting and perplexed
With this dread paper! How to act I know not;
Should I retain it, should I forward it?

[To BURLEIGH, who enters.

Oh! I am glad that you are come, my lord,
'Tis you who have preferred me to this charge;
Now free me from it, for I undertook it,
Unknowing how responsible it made me.
Let me then seek again the obscurity
In which you found me; this is not my place.

BURLEIGH.
How now? Take courage, sir! Where is the warrant?
The queen was with you.

DAVISON.
            She has quitted me
In bitter anger. Oh, advise me, help me,
Save me from this fell agony of doubt!
My lord, here is the warrant: it is signed!

BURLEIGH.

Indeed! Oh, give it, give it me!

DAVISON.
>I may not.

BURLEIGH.
How!

DAVISON.
She has not yet explained her final will.

BURLEIGH.
Explained! She has subscribed it;--give it to me.

DAVISON.
I am to execute it, and I am not.
Great heavens! I know not what I am to do!

BURLEIGH (urging more violently).
It must be now, this moment, executed.
The warrant, sir. You're lost if you delay.

DAVISON.
So am I also if I act too rashly.

BURLEIGH.
What strange infatuation. Give it me.

  [Snatches the paper from him, and exit with it.

DAVISON.
What would you? Hold? You will be my destruction.

ACT V.

SCENE I.

The Scene the same as in the First Act.

HANNAH KENNEDY in deep mourning, her eyes still red from weeping, in great but quiet anguish, is employed in sealing letters and parcels. Her sorrow often interrupts her occupation, and she is seen at such intervals to pray in silence. PAULET and DRURY, also in mourning, enter, followed by many servants, who bear golden and silver vessels, mirrors, paintings, and other valuables, and fill the back part of the stage with them. PAULET delivers to the NURSE a box of jewels and a paper, and seems to inform her by signs that it contains the inventory of the effects the QUEEN had brought with her. At the sight of these riches, the anguish of the NURSE is renewed; she sinks into a deep, glowing melancholy, during which DRURY, PAULET, and the servants silently retire.

MELVIL enters.

KENNEDY (screams aloud as soon as she observes him).
Melvil! Is it you? Behold I you again?

MELVIL.

Yes, faithful Kennedy, we meet once more.

KENNEDY.
After this long, long, painful separation!

MELVIL.
A most unhappy, bitter meeting this!

KENNEDY.
You come----

MELVIL.
    To take an everlasting leave
Of my dear queen--to bid a last farewell!

KENNEDY.
And now at length, now on the fatal morn
Which brings her death, they grant our royal lady
The presence of her friends. Oh, worthy sir,
I will not question you, how you have fared,
Nor tell you all the sufferings we've endured,
Since you were torn away from us: alas!
There will be time enough for that hereafter.
O, Melvil, Melvil, why was it our fate
To see the dawn of this unhappy day?

MELVIL.
Let us not melt each other with our grief.
Throughout my whole remaining life, as long
As ever it may be, I'll sit and weep;
A smile shall never more light up these cheeks,
Ne'er will I lay this sable garb aside,
But lead henceforth a life of endless mourning.

Yet on this last sad day I will be firm;
Pledge me your word to moderate your grief;
And when the rest of comfort all bereft,
Abandoned to despair, wail round her, we
Will lead her with heroic resolution,
And be her staff upon the road to death!

KENNEDY.
Melvil! You are deceived if you suppose
The queen has need of our support to meet
Her death with firmness. She it is, my friend,
Who will exhibit the undaunted heart.
Oh! trust me, Mary Stuart will expire
As best becomes a heroine and queen!

MELVIL.
Received she firmly, then, the sad decree
Of death?--'tis said that she was not prepared.

KENNEDY.
She was not; yet they were far other terrors
Which made our lady shudder: 'twas not death,
But her deliverer, which made her tremble.
Freedom was promised us; this very night
Had Mortimer engaged to bear us hence:
And thus the queen, perplexed 'twixt hope and fear,
And doubting still if she should trust her honor
And royal person to the adventurous youth,
Sat waiting for the morning. On a sudden
We hear a boisterous tumult in the castle;
Our ears are startled by repeated blows
Of many hammers, and we think we hear
The approach of our deliverers: hope salutes us,

And suddenly and unresisted wakes
The sweet desire of life. And now at once
The portals are thrown open--it is Paulet,
Who comes to tell us--that--the carpenters
Erect beneath our feet the murderous scaffold!

[She turns aside, overpowered by excessive anguish.

MELVIL.
O God in Heaven! Oh, tell me then how bore
The queen this terrible vicissitude?

KENNEDY (after a pause, in which she has somewhat collected herself).
Not by degrees can we relinquish life;
Quick, sudden, in the twinkling of an eye,
The separation must be made, the change
From temporal to eternal life; and God
Imparted to our mistress at this moment
His grace, to cast away each earthly hope,
And firm and full of faith to mount the skies.
No sign of pallid fear dishonored her;
No word of mourning, 'till she heard the tidings
Of Leicester's shameful treachery, the sad fate
Of the deserving youth, who sacrificed
Himself for her; the deep, the bitter anguish
Of that old knight, who lost, through her, his last,
His only hope; till then she shed no tear--
'Twas then her tears began to flow, 'twas not
Her own, but others' woe which wrung them from her.

MELVIL.
Where is she now? Can you not lead me to her?

KENNEDY.
She spent the last remainder of the night
In prayer, and from her dearest friends she took
Her last farewell in writing: then she wrote
Her will [1] with her own hand. She now enjoys
A moment of repose, the latest slumber
Refreshes her weak spirits.

MELVIL.
      Who attends her?

KENNEDY.
None but her women and physician Burgoyn:
You seem to look around you with surprise;
Your eyes appear to ask me what should mean
This show of splendor in the house of death.
Oh, sir, while yet we lived we suffered want;
But at our death plenty returns to us.

SCENE II.

  Enter MARGARET CURL.

KENNEDY.
How, madam, fares the queen? Is she awake?

CURL (drying her tears).
She is already dressed--she asks for you.

KENNEDY.
I go:--

[To MELVIL, who seems to wish to accompany her.
  But follow not until the queen
Has been prepared to see you.

    [Exit.

CURL.
    Melvil, sure,
The ancient steward?

MELVIL.
    Yes, the same.

CURL.
    Oh, sir,
This is a house which needs no steward now!
Melvil, you come from London; can you give
No tidings of my husband?

MELVIL.
    It is said
He will be set at liberty as soon----

CURL.
As soon as our dear queen shall be no more.
Oh, the unworthy, the disgraceful traitor!
He is our lady's murderer--'tis said
It was his testimony which condemned him.

MELVIL.
'Tis true.

CURL.

Oh, curse upon him! Be his soul
Condemned forever! he has borne false witness.

MELVIL.
Think, madam, what you say.

CURL.
    I will maintain it
With every sacred oath before the court,
I will repeat it in his very face;
The world shall hear of nothing else. I say
That she dies innocent!

MELVIL..
    God grant it true!

[1] The document is now in the British Museum.

SCENE III.

  Enter HANNAH KENNEDY.

KENNEDY (to CURL).
Go, madam, and require a cup of wine--
'Tis for our lady.

MELVIL.
    Is the queen then sick?

KENNEDY.

She thinks that she is strong; she is deceived
By her heroic courage; she believes
She has no need of nourishment; yet still
A hard and painful task's allotted her.
Her enemies shall not enjoy the triumph;
They shall not say that fear hath blanched her cheeks
When her fatigues have conquered human weakness.

MELVIL.
May I approach her?

KENNEDY.
    She will come herself.

SCENE IV.

  Enter BURGOYN; two women of the chamber follow him, weeping, and in deep mourning.

BURGOYN.
Oh, Melvil!

MELVIL.
    Oh, Burgoyn!

[They embrace silently.

FIRST WOMAN (to the NURSE).
    She chose to be
Alone: she wishes, at this awful moment,
For the last time, to commune with her God.

SCENE V.

Enter MARGARET CURL, bearing a golden cup of wine;
she places it hastily upon the table, and leans,
pale and trembling, against a chair.

MELVIL.
How, madam! What has frightened you?

KENNEDY.
  Oh God!

BURGOYN.
Speak, madam!

CURL.
 What, alas! have I beheld!

MELVIL.
Come to yourself, and say what you have seen!

CURL.
As I went down the staircase which conducts
To the great hall below, a door stood open;
I looked into the chamber, and I saw--
Oh heaven!

MELVIL.
 What saw you?

CURL.
 All the walls were hung

With black; a spacious scaffold, too, o'erspread
With sable cloth, was raised above the floor,
And in the middle of the scaffold stood
A dreadful sable block! upon it lay
A naked, polished axe:--the hall was full
Of cruel people, crowding round the scaffold
Who, with a horrid thirst for human blood,
Seemed waiting for the victim!

THE WOMEN.
        Gracious heaven,
Protect our queen!

MELVIL.
        Be calm; the queen approaches.

SCENE VI.

    Enter MARY in white and sumptuously arrayed, as
    for a festival: she wears hanging from her neck,
    on a row of small beads, an Agnus Dei; a rosary
    hangs from her girdle; she bears a crucifix in
    her hand, and a diadem of precious stones binds
    her hair; her large black veil is thrown back.
    On her entrance all present fall back on both sides
    with the most violent expressions of anguish.
    MELVIL falls involuntarily upon his knees.

MARY (with quiet majesty, looking round the whole circle).
Why these complaints? Why weep ye? Ye should rather
Rejoice with me, that now at length the end

Of my long woe approaches; that my shackles
Fall off, my prison opens, and my soul
Delighted mounts on seraph's wings, and seeks
The land of everlasting liberty.
When I was offered up to the oppression
Of my proud enemy, was forced to suffer
Ignoble taunts, and insults most unfitting
A free and sovereign queen, then was the time
To weep for me; but as an earnest friend,
Beneficent and healing death approaches.
All the indignities which I have suffered
On earth are covered by his sable wings.
The most degraded criminal's ennobled
By his last sufferings, by his final exit;
I feel again the crown upon my brows.
And dignity possess my swelling soul!

[Advancing a few steps.

How! Melvil here! My worthy sir, not so;
Arise; you rather come in time to see
The triumph of your mistress than her death.
One comfort, which I never had expected,
Is granted me, that after death my name
Will not be quite abandoned to my foes;
One friend at least, one partner of my faith,
Will be my witness in the hour of death.
Say, honest Melvil, how you fared the while
In this inhospitable, hostile land?
For since the time they tore you from my side
My fears for you have oft depressed my soul.

MELVIL.

No other evil galled me but my grief
For thee, and that I wanted power to serve thee.

MARY.
How fares my chamberlain, old Didier?
But sure the faithful servant long has slept
The sleep of death, for he was full of years.

MELVIL.
God hath not granted him as yet this grace;
He lives to see the grave o'erwhelm thy youth.

MARY.
Oh! could I but have felt before my death,
The happiness of pressing one descendant
Of the dear blood of Stuart to my bosom.
But I must suffer in a foreign land,
None but my servants to bewail my fate!
Sir; to your loyal bosom I commit
My latest wishes. Bear then, sir, my blessing
To the most Christian king, my royal brother,
And the whole royal family of France.
I bless the cardinal, my honored uncle,
And also Henry Guise, my noble cousin.
I bless the holy father, the vicegerent
Of Christ on earth, who will, I trust, bless me.
I bless the King of Spain, who nobly offered
Himself as my deliverer, my avenger.
They are remembered in my will: I hope
That they will not despise, how poor soe'er
They be, the presents of a heart which loves them.

[Turning to her servants.

I have bequeathed you to my royal brother
Of France; he will protect you, he will give you
Another country, and a better home;
And if my last desire have any weight,
Stay not in England; let no haughty Briton
Glut his proud heart with your calamities,
Nor see those in the dust who once were mine.
Swear by this image of our suffering Lord
To leave this fatal land when I'm no more.

MELVIL (touching the crucifix).
I swear obedience in the name of all.

MARY.
What I, though poor and plundered, still possess,
Of which I am allowed to make disposal,
Shall be amongst you shared; for I have hope
In this at least my will may be fulfilled.
And what I wear upon my way to death
Is yours--nor envy me on this occasion
The pomp of earth upon the road to heaven.

   [To the ladies of her chamber.

To you, my Alice, Gertrude, Rosamund,
I leave my pearls, my garments: you are young,
And ornament may still delight your hearts.
You, Margaret, possess the nearest claims,
To you I should be generous: for I leave you
The most unhappy woman of them all.
That I have not avenged your husband's fault
On you I hope my legacy will prove.

The worth of gold, my Hannah, charms not thee;
Nor the magnificence of precious stones:
My memory, I know, will be to thee
The dearest jewel; take this handkerchief,
I worked it for thee, in the hours of sorrow,
With my own hands, and my hot, scalding tears
Are woven in the texture:--you will bind
My eyes with this, when it is time: this last
Sad service I would wish but from my Hannah.

KENNEDY.
O Melvil! I cannot support it.

MARY.
        Come,
Come all and now receive my last farewell.

  [She stretches forth her hands; the WOMEN
  violently weeping, fall successively at her feet,
  and kiss her outstretched hand.

Margaret, farewell--my Alice, fare thee well;
Thanks, Burgoyn, for thy honest, faithful service--
Thy lips are hot, my Gertrude:--I have been
Much hated, yet have been as much beloved.
May a deserving husband bless my Gertrude,
For this warm, glowing heart is formed for love.
Bertha, thy choice is better, thou hadst rather
Become the chaste and pious bride of heaven;
Oh! haste thee to fulfil thy vows; the goods
Of earth are all deceitful; thou may'st learn
This lesson from thy queen. No more; farewell,
Farewell, farewell, my friends, farewell for ever.

[*She turns suddenly from them; all but* MELVIL *retire at different sides.*

SCENE VII.

MARY, MELVIL.

MARY (*after the others are all gone*).
I have arranged all temporal concerns,
And hope to leave the world in debt to none;
Melvil, one thought alone there is which binds
My troubled soul, nor suffers it to fly
Delighted and at liberty to heaven.

MELVIL.
Disclose it to me; ease your bosom, trust
Your doubts, your sorrows, to your faithful friend.

MARY.
I see eternity's abyss before me;
Soon must I stand before the highest Judge,
And have not yet appeased the Holy One.
A priest of my religion is denied me,
And I disdain to take the sacrament,
The holy, heavenly nourishment, from priests
Of a false faith; I die in the belief
Of my own church, for that alone can save.

MELVIL.
Compose your heart; the fervent, pious wish

Is prized in heaven as high as the performance.
The might of tyrants can but bind the hands,
The heart's devotion rises free to God,
The word is dead--'tis faith which brings to life.

MARY.
The heart is not sufficient of itself;
Our faith must have some earthly pledge to ground
Its claim to the high bliss of heaven. For this
Our God became incarnate, and enclosed
Mysteriously his unseen heavenly grace
Within an outward figure of a body.
The church it is, the holy one, the high one,
Which rears for us the ladder up to heaven:--
'Tis called the Catholic Apostolic church,--
For 'tis but general faith can strengthen faith;
Where thousands worship and adore the heat
Breaks out in flame, and, borne on eagle wings,
The soul mounts upwards to the heaven of heavens.
Ah! happy they, who for the glad communion
Of pious prayer meet in the house of God!
The altar is adorned, the tapers blaze,
The bell invites, the incense soars on high;
The bishop stands enrobed, he takes the cup,
And blessing it declares the solemn mystery,
The transformation of the elements;
And the believing people fall delighted
To worship and adore the present Godhead.
Alas! I only am debarred from this;
The heavenly benediction pierces not
My prison walls: its comfort is denied me.

MELVIL.

Yes! it can pierce them--put thy trust in Him
Who is almighty--in the hand of faith,
The withered staff can send forth verdant branches
And he who from the rock called living water,
He can prepare an altar in this prison,
Can change----
   [Seizing the cup, which stands upon the table.
     The earthly contents of this cup
Into a substance of celestial grace.

MARY.
Melvil! Oh, yes, I understand you, Melvil!
Here is no priest, no church, no sacrament;
But the Redeemer says, "When two or three
Are in my name assembled, I am with them,"
What consecrates the priest? Say, what ordains him
To be the Lord's interpreter? a heart
Devoid of guile, and a reproachless conduct.
Well, then, though unordained, be you my priest;
To you will I confide my last confession,
And take my absolution from your lips.

MELVIL.
If then thy heart be with such zeal inflamed,
I tell thee that for thine especial comfort,
The Lord may work a miracle. Thou say'st
Here is no priest, no church, no sacrament--
Thou err'st--here is a priest--here is a God;
A God descends to thee in real presence.

   [At these words he uncovers his head,
   and shows a host in a golden vessel.

I am a priest--to hear thy last confession,
And to announce to thee the peace of God
Upon thy way to death. I have received
Upon my head the seven consecrations.
I bring thee, from his Holiness, this host,
Which, for thy use, himself has deigned to bless.

MARY.
Is then a heavenly happiness prepared
To cheer me on the very verge of death?
As an immortal one on golden clouds
Descends, as once the angel from on high,
Delivered the apostle from his fetters:--
He scorns all bars, he scorns the soldier's sword,
He steps undaunted through the bolted portals,
And fills the dungeon with his native glory;
Thus here the messenger of heaven appears
When every earthly champion had deceived me.
And you, my servant once, are now the servant
Of the Most High, and his immortal Word!
As before me your knees were wont to bend,
Before you humbled, now I kiss the dust.

   [She sinks before him on her knees.

MELVIL (making over her the sign of the cross).
Hear, Mary, Queen of Scotland:--in the name
Of God the Father, Son, and Holy Ghost,
Hast thou examined carefully thy heart,
Swearest thou, art thou prepared in thy confession
To speak the truth before the God of truth?

MARY.

Before my God and thee, my heart lies open.

MELVIL.
What calls thee to the presence of the Highest?

MARY.
I humbly do acknowledge to have erred
Most grievously, I tremble to approach,
Sullied with sin, the God of purity.

MELVIL.
Declare the sin which weighs so heavily
Upon thy conscience since thy last confession.

MARY.
My heart was filled with thoughts of envious hate,
And vengeance took possession of my bosom.
I hope forgiveness of my sins from God,
Yet could I not forgive my enemy.

MELVIL.
Repentest thou of the sin? Art thou, in sooth,
Resolved to leave this world at peace with all?

MARY.
As surely as I wish the joys of heaven.

MELVIL.
What other sin hath armed thy heart against thee?

MARY.
Ah! not alone through hate; through lawless love
Have I still more abused the sovereign good.

My heart was vainly turned towards the man
Who left me in misfortune, who deceived me.

MELVIL.
Repentest thou of the sin? And hast thou turned
Thy heart, from this idolatry, to God?

MARY.
It was the hardest trial I have passed;
This last of earthly bonds is torn asunder.

MELVIL.
What other sin disturbs thy guilty conscience?

MARY.
A bloody crime, indeed of ancient date,
And long ago confessed; yet with new terrors.
It now attacks me, black and grisly steps
Across my path, and shuts the gates of heaven:
By my connivance fell the king, my husband--
I gave my hand and heart to a seducer--
By rigid penance I have made atonement;
Yet in my soul the worm is gnawing still.

MELVIL.
Has then thy heart no other accusation,
Which hath not been confessed and washed away?

MARY.
All you have heard with which my heart is charged.

MELVIL.
Think on the presence of Omniscience;

Think on the punishments with which the church
Threatens imperfect and reserved confessions
This is the sin to everlasting death,
For this is sinning 'gainst his Holy Spirit.

MARY.
So may eternal grace with victory
Crown my last contest, as I wittingly
Have nothing hid----

MELVIL.
    How? Wilt thou then conceal
The crime from God for which thou art condemned?
Thou tell'st me nothing of the share thou hadst
In Babington and Parry's bloody treason:
Thou diest for this a temporal death; for this
Wilt thou, too, die the everlasting death?

MARY.
I am prepared to meet eternity;
Within the narrow limits of an hour
I shall appear before my Judge's throne.
But, I repeat it, my confession's ended.

MELVIL.
Consider well--the heart is a deceiver.
Thou hast, perhaps, with sly equivocation,
The word avoided, which would make thee guilty
Although thy will was party to the crime.
Remember, that no juggler's tricks can blind
The eye of fire which darts through every breast.

MARY.

'Tis true that I have called upon all princes
To free me from unworthy chains; yet 'tis
As true that, neither by intent or deed,
Have I attempted my oppressor's life.

MELVIL.
Your secretaries then have witnessed falsely.

MARY.
It is as I have said;--what they have witnessed
The Lord will judge.

MELVIL.
    Thou mountest, then, satisfied
Of thy own innocence, the fatal scaffold?

MARY.
God suffers me in mercy to atone,
By undeserved death, my youth's transgressions.

MELVIL (making over her the sign of the cross).
Go, then, and expiate them all by death;
Sink a devoted victim on the altar,
Thus shall thy blood atone the blood thou'st spilt.
From female frailty were derived thy faults,
Free from the weakness of mortality,
The spotless spirit seeks the blest abodes.
Now, then, by the authority which God
Hath unto me committed, I absolve thee
From all thy sins; be as thy faith thy welfare!

  [He gives her the host.

Receive the body which for thee was offered--

> [He takes the cup which stands upon the table,
> consecrates it with silent prayer, then presents
> it to her; she hesitates to take it, and makes
> signs to him to withdraw it.

Receive the blood which for thy sins was shed,
Receive it; 'tis allowed thee by the pope
To exercise in death the highest office
Of kings, the holy office of the priesthood.

> [She takes the cup.

And as thou now, in this his earthly body
Hast held with God mysterious communion,
So may'st thou henceforth, in his realm of joy,
Where sin no more exists, nor tears of woe,
A fair, transfigured spirit, join thyself
Forever with the Godhead, and forever.

> [He sets down the cup; hearing a noise,
> he covers his head, and goes to the door;
> MARY remains in silent devotion on her knees.

MELVIL (returning).
A painful conflict is in store for thee.
Feel'st thou within thee strength enough to smother
Each impulse of malignity and hate?

MARY.
I fear not a relapse. I have to God
Devoted both my hatred and my love.

MELVIL.
Well, then, prepare thee to receive my Lords
Of Leicester and of Burleigh. They are here.

SCENE VIII.

Enter BURLEIGH, LEICESTER, and PAULET.

[LEICESTER remains in the background, without raising his eyes; BURLEIGH, who remarks his confusion, steps between him and the QUEEN.

BURLEIGH.
I come, my Lady Stuart, to receive
Your last commands and wishes.

MARY.
      Thanks, my lord.

BURLEIGH.
It is the pleasure of my royal mistress
That nothing reasonable be denied you.

MARY.
My will, my lord, declares my last desires;
I've placed it in the hand of Sir Amias,
And humbly beg that it may be fulfilled.

PAULET.
You may rely on this.

MARY.
>I beg that all
My servants unmolested may return
To France, or Scotland, as their wishes lead.

BURLEIGH.
It shall be as you wish.

MARY.
>And since my body
Is not to rest in consecrated ground,
I pray you suffer this my faithful servant
To bear my heart to France, to my relations--
Alas! 'twas ever there.

BURLEIGH.
>It shall be done.
What wishes else?

MARY.
>Unto her majesty
Of England bear a sister's salutation;
Tell her that from the bottom of my heart
I pardon her my death; most humbly, too,
I crave her to forgive me for the passion
With which I spoke to her. May God preserve her
And bless her with a long and prosperous reign.

BURLEIGH.
Say, do you still adhere to your resolve,
And still refuse assistance from the dean?

MARY.
My lord, I've made my peace with God.

[To PAULET.

      Good sir,
I have unwittingly caused you much sorrow,
Bereft you of your age's only stay.
Oh, let me hope you do not hate my name.

PAULET (giving her his hand).
The Lord be with you! Go your way in peace.

SCENE IX.

    HANNAH KENNEDY, and the other women of the QUEEN crowd
    into the room with marks of horror. The SHERIFF follows
    them, a white staff in his hand; behind are seen, through
    the open doors, men under arms.

MARY.
What ails thee, Hannah? Yes, my hour is come.
The sheriff comes to lead me to my fate,
And part we must. Farewell!

KENNEDY and CURL.
    We will not leave thee,
We will not part from thee.

MARY (to MELVIL).
    You, worthy sir,

And my dear, faithful Hannah, shall attend me
In my last moments. I am sure, my lord
Will not refuse my heart this consolation.

BURLEIGH.
For this I have no warrant.

MARY.
      How, my lord;
Can you deny me, then, this small petition?
Respect my sex; who shall attend me else,
And yield me the last service? Sure, it never
Can be my sister's pleasure that in me
My sex should be insulted; that these men
With their rude hands should touch my royal person.

BURLEIGH.
'Tis ordered that no woman shall ascend
The scaffold steps with you. Their tears and moans----

MARY.
She shall not weep, my lord; she shall not moan;
I answer for my Hannah's resolution;
Be merciful; divide me not so soon
From my true foster-mother, from my friend.
She bore me on her arms into this life;
Let her then gently lead me to my death.

PAULET (to BURLEIGH).
Yield to her wishes.

BURLEIGH.
      Be it so.

MARY.
>I now
Have nothing in this world to wish for more.

[She takes the crucifix, and kisses it.

My God! My Comforter! My blest Redeemer!
As once thy arms were stretched upon the cross,
Let them be now extended to receive me!

[She turns round to go; at the same moment her
eyes fall upon LEICESTER, who, on her going, starts
involuntarily, and turns his eyes towards her; at
this sight MARY trembles, her knees fail her, she is
about to fall, when LEICESTER catches at her, and
receives her in his arms; she regards him for some
time earnestly, and in silence; he cannot support her
looks; at length she speaks.

You keep your word, my Lord of Leicester: for
You promised me your arm to lead me forth
From prison, and you lend it to me now.
At length the wished-for day is come, and what
Was oft the object of my fondest dreams
Is now accomplished: and the Earl of Leicester,
The long-expected, the long-wished-for friend,
Appears at length in Fotheringay Castle.
I see him standing in my prison; all
Is ready for the journey; all the gates
Stand open, and at length I cross the threshold,
Conducted by his hand; and now I leave
These dismal walls behind me, and forever.

All is fulfilled, and you have saved your honor.

[He stands as if annihilated; she continues,
with a gentle voice.

Yes, Leicester; not for liberty alone
I wished to be indebted to your hands.
You should have made me bless that liberty.
Led by your hand, and happy in your love,
I hoped once more to taste the joys of life.
Yes; now that I'm prepared from all the world
To part, and to become a happy spirit,
Whom earthly inclinations tempt no more!
Now, Leicester, I may venture to confess
Without a blush the frailty I have conquered;
Farewell, my lord; and, if you can, be happy!
To woo two queens has been your daring aim;
You have disdained a tender, loving heart,
Betrayed it in the hope to win a proud one:
Kneel at the feet of Queen Elizabeth!
May your reward not prove your punishment.
Farewell; I now have nothing more on earth.

[She goes, preceded by the SHERIFF; at her side
MELVIL and her nurse; BURLEIGH and PAULET follow;
the others, wailing, follow her with their eyes
till she disappears; they then retire through the
other two doors.

SCENE X.

LEICESTER (remaining alone).
Do I live still? Can I still bear to live?
Will not this roof fall down and bury me?
Yawns no abyss to swallow in its gulf
The veriest wretch on earth? What have I lost?
Oh, what a pearl have I not cast away!
What bliss celestial madly dashed aside!
She's gone, a spirit purged from earthly stain,
And the despair of hell remains for me!
Where is the purpose now with which I came
To stifle my heart's voice in callous scorn?
To see her head descend upon the block
With unaverted and indifferent eyes?
How doth her presence wake my slumbering shame?
Must she in death surround me with love's toils?
Lost, wretched man! No more it suits thee now
To melt away in womanly compassion:
Love's golden bliss lies not upon thy path,
Then arm thy breast in panoply of steel,
And henceforth be thy brows of adamant!
Wouldst thou not lose the guerdon of thy guilt,
Thou must uphold, complete it daringly!
Pity be dumb; mine eyes be petrified!
I'll see--I will be witness of her fall.

[He advances with resolute steps towards the door
through which MARY passed; but stops suddenly half way.

No! No! The terrors of all hell possess me.
I cannot look upon the dreadful deed;
I cannot see her die! Hark! What was that?

They are already there. Beneath my feet
The bloody business is preparing. Hark!
I hear their voices. Hence! Away, away
From this abode of misery and death!

  [He attempts to escape by another door;
    finds it locked, and returns.

How! Does some demon chain me to this spot?
To hear what I would shudder to behold?
That voice--it is the dean's, exhorting her;
She interrupts him. Hark--she prays aloud;
Her voice is firm--now all is still, quite still!
And sobs and women's moans are all I hear.
Now, they undress her; they remove the stool;
She kneels upon the cushion; lays her head----

  [Having spoken these last words, and paused awhile,
    he is seen with a convulsive motion suddenly to shrink
    and faint away; a confused hum of voices is heard at
    the same moment from below, and continues for some time.

SCENE XI.

  The Second Chamber in the Fourth Act.

ELIZABETH (entering from a side door; her gait and action expressive
    of the most violent uneasiness).
No message yet arrived! What! no one here!
Will evening never come! Stands the sun still
In its ethereal course? I can no more

Remain upon the rack of expectation!
Is it accomplished? Is it not? I shudder
At both events, and do not dare to ask.
My Lord of Leicester comes not,--Burleigh too,
Whom I appointed to fulfil the sentence.
If they have quitted London then 'tis done,
The bolt has left its rest--it cuts the air--
It strikes; has struck already: were my realm
At stake I could not now arrest its course.
Who's there?

SCENE XII.

   Enter a PAGE.

ELIZABETH.
Returned alone? Where are the lords?

PAGE.
My Lord High-Treasurer and the Earl of Leicester?

ELIZABETH.
Where are they?

PAGE.
     They are not in London.

ELIZABETH.
        No!
Where are they then?

PAGE.
>That no one could inform me;
Before the dawn, mysteriously, in haste
They quitted London.

ELIZABETH (exultingly).
>I am Queen of England!

[Walking up and down in the greatest agitation.

Go--call me--no, remain, boy! She is dead;
Now have I room upon the earth at last.
Why do I shake? Whence comes this aguish dread?
My fears are covered by the grave; who dares
To say I did it? I have tears enough
In store to weep her fall. Are you still here?
>[To the PAGE.
Command my secretary, Davison,
To come to me this instant. Let the Earl
Of Shrewsbury be summoned. Here he comes.

>[Exit PAGE.

SCENE XIII.

Enter SHREWSBURY.

ELIZABETH.
Welcome, my noble lord. What tidings; say
It cannot be a trifle which hath led
Your footsteps hither at so late an hour.

SHREWSBURY.
My liege, the doubts that hung upon my heart,
And dutiful concern for your fair fame,
Directed me this morning to the Tower,
Where Mary's secretaries, Nau and Curl,
Are now confined as prisoners, for I wished
Once more to put their evidence to proof.
On my arrival the lieutenant seemed
Embarrassed and perplexed; refused to show me
His prisoners; but my threats obtained admittance.
God! what a sight was there! With frantic looks,
With hair dishevelled, on his pallet lay
The Scot like one tormented by a fury.
The miserable man no sooner saw me
Than at my feet he fell, and there, with screams,
Clasping my knees, and writhing like a worm,
Implored, conjured me to acquaint him with
His sovereign's destiny, for vague reports
Had somehow reached the dungeons of the Tower
That she had been condemned to suffer death.
When I confirmed these tidings, adding, too,
That on his evidence she had been doomed,--
He started wildly up,--caught by the throat
His fellow-prisoner; with the giant strength
Of madness tore him to the ground and tried
To strangle him. No sooner had we saved
The wretch from his fierce grapple than at once
He turned his rage against himself and beat
His breast with savage fists; then cursed himself
And his companions to the depths of hell!
His evidence was false; the fatal letters
To Babington, which he had sworn were true,

He now denounced as forgeries; for he
Had set down words the queen had never spoken;
The traitor Nau had led him to this treason.
Then ran he to the casement, threw it wide
With frantic force, and cried into the street
So loud that all the people gathered round:
I am the man, Queen Mary's secretary,
The traitor who accused his mistress falsely;
I bore false witness and am cursed forever!

ELIZABETH.
You said yourself that he had lost his wits;
A madman's words prove nothing.

SHREWSBURY.
      Yet this madness
Serves in itself to swell the proof. My liege,
Let me conjure thee; be not over-hasty;
Prithee, give order for a new inquiry!

ELIZABETH.
I will, my lord, because it is your wish,
Not that I can believe my noble peers
Have in this case pronounced a hasty judgment.
To set your mind at rest the inquiry shall
Be straight renewed. Well that 'tis not too late!
Upon the honor of our royal name,
No, not the shadow of a doubt shall rest.

SCENE XIV.

  Enter DAVISON.

ELIZABETH.
The sentence, sir, which I but late intrusted
Unto your keeping; where is it?

DAVISON (in the utmost astonishment).
        The sentence!

ELIZABETH (more urgent).
Which yesterday I gave into your charge.

DAVISON.
Into my charge, my liege!

ELIZABETH.
      The people urged
And baited me to sign it. I perforce
Was driven to yield obedience to their will.
I did so; did so on extreme constraint,
And in your hands deposited the paper.
To gain time was my purpose; you remember
What then I told you. Now, the paper, sir!

SHREWSBURY.
Restore it, sir, affairs have changed since then,
The inquiry must be set on foot anew.

DAVISON.
Anew! Eternal mercy!

ELIZABETH.
>Why this pause,
This hesitation? Where, sir, is the paper?

DAVISON.
I am undone! Undone! My fate is sealed!

ELIZABETH (interrupting him violently).
Let me not fancy, sir----

DAVISON.
>Oh, I am lost!
I have it not.

ELIZABETH.
>How? What?

SHREWSBURY.
>Oh, God in heaven!

DAVISON.
It is in Burleigh's hands--since yesterday.

ELIZABETH.
Wretch! Is it thus you have obeyed my orders?
Did I not lay my strict injunction on you
To keep it carefully?

DAVISON.
>No such injunction
Was laid on me, my liege.

ELIZABETH.
>Give me the lie?
Opprobrious wretch! When did I order you
To give the paper into Burleigh's hands?

DAVISON.
Never expressly in so many words.

ELIZABETH.
And, paltering villain I dare you then presume
To construe, as you list, my words--and lay
Your bloody meaning on them? Wo betide you,
If evil come of this officious deed!
Your life shall answer the event to me.
Earl Shrewsbury, you see how my good name
Has been abused!

SHREWSBURY.
>I see! Oh, God in heaven!

ELIZABETH.
What say you?

SHREWSBURY.
>If the knight has dared to act
In this, upon his own authority,
Without the knowledge of your majesty,
He must be cited to the Court of Peers
To answer there for subjecting thy name
To the abhorrence of all after time.

SCENE XV.

   Enter BURLEIGH.

BURLEIGH (bowing his knee before the QUEEN).
Long life and glory to my royal mistress,
And may all enemies of her dominions
End like this Stuart.

   [SHREWSBURY hides his face. DAVIDSON wrings his hands in despair.

ELIZABETH.
     Speak, my lord; did you
From me receive the warrant?

BURLEIGH.
     No, my queen;
From Davison.

ELIZABETH.
    And did he in my name
Deliver it?

BURLEIGH.
   No, that I cannot say.

ELIZABETH.
And dared you then to execute the writ
Thus hastily, nor wait to know my pleasure?
Just was the sentence--we are free from blame
Before the world; yet it behooved thee not
To intercept our natural clemency.
For this, my lord, I banish you my presence;

And as this forward will was yours alone
Bear you alone the curse of the misdeed!

[To DAVISON.

For you, sir; who have traitorously o'erstepped
The bounds of your commission, and betrayed
A sacred pledge intrusted to your care,
A more severe tribunal is prepared:
Let him be straight conducted to the Tower,
And capital arraignments filed against him.
My honest Talbot, you alone have proved,
'Mongst all my counsellors, an upright man:
You shall henceforward be my guide--my friend.

SHREWSBURY.
Oh! banish not the truest of your friends;
Nor cast those into prison, who for you
Have acted; who for you are silent now.
But suffer me, great queen, to give the seal,
Which, these twelve years, I've borne unworthily,
Back to your royal hands, and take my leave.

ELIZABETH (surprised).
No, Shrewsbury; you surely would not now
Desert me? No; not now.

SHREWSBURY.
    Pardon, I am
Too old, and this right hand is growing too stiff
To set the seal upon your later deeds.

ELIZABETH.

Will he forsake me, who has saved my life?

SHREWSBURY.
'Tis little I have done: I could not save
Your nobler part. Live--govern happily!
Your rival's dead! Henceforth you've nothing more
To fear--henceforth to nothing pay regard.

    [Exit.

ELIZABETH (to the EARL of KENT, who enters).
Send for the Earl of Leicester.

KENT.
    He desires
To be excused--he is embarked for France.

    The Curtain drops.

www.bookjungle.com *email: sales@bookjungle.com fax: 630-214-0564 mail: Book Jungle PO Box 2226 Champaign, IL 61825*

The Codes Of Hammurabi And Moses
W. W. Davies

QTY

The discovery of the Hammurabi Code is one of the greatest achievements of archaeology, and is of paramount interest, not only to the student of the Bible, but also to all those interested in ancient history...

Religion   **ISBN:** *1-59462-338-4*   Pages:132
MSRP *$12.95*

The Theory of Moral Sentiments
Adam Smith

QTY

This work from 1749. contains original theories of conscience amd moral judgment and it is the foundation for systemof morals.

Philosophy   ISBN: *1-59462-777-0*   Pages:536
MSRP *$19.95*

Jessica's First Prayer
Hesba Stretton

QTY

In a screened and secluded corner of one of the many railway-bridges which span the streets of London there could be seen a few years ago, from five o'clock every morning until half past eight, a tidily set-out coffee-stall, consisting of a trestle and board, upon which stood two large tin cans, with a small fire of charcoal burning under each so as to keep the coffee boiling during the early hours of the morning when the work-people were thronging into the city on their way to their daily toil...

Childrens   ISBN: *1-59462-373-2*   Pages:84
MSRP *$9.95*

My Life and Work
Henry Ford

QTY

Henry Ford revolutionized the world with his implementation of mass production for the Model T automobile. Gain valuable business insight into his life and work with his own auto-biography... "We have only started on our development of our country we have not as yet, with all our talk of wonderful progress, done more than scratch the surface. The progress has been wonderful enough but..."

Biographies/   ISBN: *1-59462-198-5*   Pages:300
MSRP *$21.95*

www.bookjungle.com *email: sales@bookjungle.com fax: 630-214-0564 mail: Book Jungle PO Box 2226 Champaign, IL 61825*

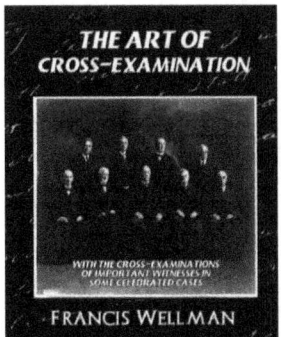

The Art of Cross-Examination
Francis Wellman

QTY

I presume it is the experience of every author, after his first book is published upon an important subject, to be almost overwhelmed with a wealth of ideas and illustrations which could readily have been included in his book, and which to his own mind, at least, seem to make a second edition inevitable. Such certainly was the case with me; and when the first edition had reached its sixth impression in five months, I rejoiced to learn that it seemed to my publishers that the book had met with a sufficiently favorable reception to justify a second and considerably enlarged edition. ...

Pages:412

Reference   ISBN: *1-59462-647-2*   *MSRP $19.95*

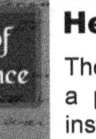

On the Duty of Civil Disobedience
Henry David Thoreau

QTY

Thoreau wrote his famous essay, On the Duty of Civil Disobedience, as a protest against an unjust but popular war and the immoral but popular institution of slave-owning. He did more than write—he declined to pay his taxes, and was hauled off to gaol in consequence. Who can say how much this refusal of his hastened the end of the war and of slavery ?

Law   ISBN: *1-59462-747-9*   **Pages:48**
MSRP $7.45

Dream Psychology Psychoanalysis for Beginners
Sigmund Freud

QTY

Sigmund Freud, born Sigismund Schlomo Freud (May 6, 1856 - September 23, 1939), was a Jewish-Austrian neurologist and psychiatrist who co-founded the psychoanalytic school of psychology. Freud is best known for his theories of the unconscious mind, especially involving the mechanism of repression; his redefinition of sexual desire as mobile and directed towards a wide variety of objects; and his therapeutic techniques, especially his understanding of transference in the therapeutic relationship and the presumed value of dreams as sources of insight into unconscious desires.

Pages:196

Psychology   ISBN: *1-59462-905-6*   *MSRP $15.45*

The Miracle of Right Thought
Orison Swett Marden

QTY

Believe with all of your heart that you will do what you were made to do. When the mind has once formed the habit of holding cheerful, happy, prosperous pictures, it will not be easy to form the opposite habit. It does not matter how improbable or how far away this realization may see, or how dark the prospects may be, if we visualize them as best we can, as vividly as possible, hold tenaciously to them and vigorously struggle to attain them, they will gradually become actualized, realized in the life. But a desire, a longing without endeavor, a yearning abandoned or held indifferently will vanish without realization.

Pages:360

Self Help   ISBN: *1-59462-644-8*   *MSRP $25.45*

www.bookjungle.com email: sales@bookjungle.com fax: 630-214-0564 mail: Book Jungle PO Box 2226 Champaign, IL 61825

QTY

	Title	ISBN	Price
☐	**The Rosicrucian Cosmo-Conception Mystic Christianity** by *Max Heindel*	ISBN: 1-59462-188-8	$38.95
	The Rosicrucian Cosmo-conception is not dogmatic, neither does it appeal to any other authority than the reason of the student. It is: not controversial, but is: sent forth in the, hope that it may help to clear...		New Age/Religion Pages 646
☐	**Abandonment To Divine Providence** by *Jean-Pierre de Caussade*	ISBN: 1-59462-228-0	$25.95
	"The Rev. Jean Pierre de Caussade was one of the most celebrated spiritual writers of the Society of Jesus in France in the 18th Century. His death took place at Toulouse in 1751. His works have gone through many editions and have been republished...		Inspirational/Religion Pages 400
☐	**Mental Chemistry** by *Charles Haanel*	ISBN: 1-59462-192-6	$23.95
	Mental Chemistry allows the change of material conditions by combining and appropriately utilizing the power of the mind. Much like applied chemistry creates something new and unique out of careful combinations of chemicals the mastery of mental chemistry...		New Age Pages 354
☐	**The Letters of Robert Browning and Elizabeth Barret Barrett 1845-1846 vol II** by *Robert Browning and Elizabeth Barrett*	ISBN: 1-59462-193-4	$35.95
			Biographies Pages 596
☐	**Gleanings In Genesis (volume I)** by *Arthur W. Pink*	ISBN: 1-59462-130-6	$27.45
	Appropriately has Genesis been termed "the seed plot of the Bible" for in it we have, in germ form, almost all of the great doctrines which are afterwards fully developed in the books of Scripture which follow...		Religion/Inspirational Pages 420
☐	**The Master Key** by *L. W. de Laurence*	ISBN: 1-59462-001-6	$30.95
	In no branch of human knowledge has there been a more lively increase of the spirit of research during the past few years than in the study of Psychology, Concentration and Mental Discipline. The requests for authentic lessons in Thought Control, Mental Discipline and...		New Age/Business Pages 422
☐	**The Lesser Key Of Solomon Goetia** by *L. W. de Laurence*	ISBN: 1-59462-092-X	$9.95
	This translation of the first book of the "Lemegton" which is now for the first time made accessible to students of Talismanic Magic was done, after careful collation and edition, from numerous Ancient Manuscripts in Hebrew, Latin, and French...		New Age/Occult Pages 92
☐	**Rubaiyat Of Omar Khayyam** by *Edward Fitzgerald*	ISBN:1-59462-332-5	$13.95
	Edward Fitzgerald, whom the world has already learned, in spite of his own efforts to remain within the shadow of anonymity, to look upon as one of the rarest poets of the century, was born at Bredfield, in Suffolk, on the 31st of March, 1809. He was the third son of John Purcell...		Music Pages 172
☐	**Ancient Law** by *Henry Maine*	ISBN: 1-59462-128-4	$29.95
	The chief object of the following pages is to indicate some of the earliest ideas of mankind, as they are reflected in Ancient Law, and to point out the relation of those ideas to modern thought.		Religiom/History Pages 452
☐	**Far-Away Stories** by *William J. Locke*	ISBN: 1-59462-129-2	$19.45
	"Good wine needs no bush, but a collection of mixed vintages does. And this book is just such a collection. Some of the stories I do not want to remain buried for ever in the museum files of dead magazine-numbers an author's not unpardonable vanity..."		Fiction Pages 272
☐	**Life of David Crockett** by *David Crockett*	ISBN: 1-59462-250-7	$27.45
	"Colonel David Crockett was one of the most remarkable men of the times in which he lived. Born in humble life, but gifted with a strong will, an indomitable courage, and unremitting perseverance...		Biographies/New Age Pages 424
☐	**Lip-Reading** by *Edward Nitchie*	ISBN: 1-59462-206-X	$25.95
	Edward B. Nitchie, founder of the New York School for the Hard of Hearing, now the Nitchie School of Lip-Reading, Inc, wrote "LIP-READING Principles and Practice". The development and perfecting of this meritorious work on lip-reading was an undertaking...		How-to Pages 400
☐	**A Handbook of Suggestive Therapeutics, Applied Hypnotism, Psychic Science** by *Henry Munro*	ISBN: 1-59462-214-0	$24.95
			Health/New Age/Health/Self-help Pages 376
☐	**A Doll's House: and Two Other Plays** by *Henrik Ibsen*	ISBN: 1-59462-112-8	$19.95
	Henrik Ibsen created this classic when in revolutionary 1848 Rome. Introducing some striking concepts in playwriting for the realist genre, this play has been studied the world over.		Fiction/Classics/Plays 308
☐	**The Light of Asia** by *sir Edwin Arnold*	ISBN: 1-59462-204-3	$13.95
	In this poetic masterpiece, Edwin Arnold describes the life and teachings of Buddha. The man who was to become known as Buddha to the world was born as Prince Gautama of India but he rejected the worldly riches and abandoned the reigns of power when...		Religion/History/Biographies Pages 170
☐	**The Complete Works of Guy de Maupassant** by *Guy de Maupassant*	ISBN: 1-59462-157-8	$16.95
	"For days and days, nights and nights, I had dreamed of that first kiss which was to consecrate our engagement, and I knew not on what spot I should put my lips..."		Fiction/Classics Pages 240
☐	**The Art of Cross-Examination** by *Francis L. Wellman*	ISBN: 1-59462-309-0	$26.95
	Written by a renowned trial lawyer, Wellman imparts his experience and uses case studies to explain how to use psychology to extract desired information through questioning.		How-to/Science/Reference Pages 408
☐	**Answered or Unanswered?** by *Louisa Vaughan* Miracles of Faith in China	ISBN: 1-59462-248-5	$10.95
			Religion Pages 112
☐	**The Edinburgh Lectures on Mental Science (1909)** by *Thomas*	ISBN: 1-59462-008-3	$11.95
	This book contains the substance of a course of lectures recently given by the writer in the Queen Street Hall, Edinburgh. Its purpose is to indicate the Natural Principles governing the relation between Mental Action and Material Conditions...		New Age/Psychology Pages 148
☐	**Ayesha** by *H. Rider Haggard*	ISBN: 1-59462-301-5	$24.95
	Verily and indeed it is the unexpected that happens! Probably if there was one person upon the earth from whom the Editor of this, and of a certain previous history, did not expect to hear again...		Classics Pages 380
☐	**Ayala's Angel** by *Anthony Trollope*	ISBN: 1-59462-352-X	$29.95
	The two girls were both pretty, but Lucy who was twenty-one who supposed to be simple and comparatively unattractive, whereas Ayala was credited, as her Bombwhat romantic name might show, with poetic charm and a taste for romance. Ayala when her father died was nineteen...		Fiction Pages 484
☐	**The American Commonwealth** by *James Bryce*	ISBN: 1-59462-286-8	$34.45
	An interpretation of American democratic political theory. It examines political mechanics and society from the perspective of Scotsman James Bryce		Politics Pages 572
☐	**Stories of the Pilgrims** by *Margaret P. Pumphrey*	ISBN: 1-59462-116-0	$17.95
	This book explores pilgrims religious oppression in England as well as their escape to Holland and eventual crossing to America on the Mayflower, and their early days in New England...		History Pages 268

www.bookjungle.com *email: sales@bookjungle.com fax: 630-214-0564 mail: Book Jungle PO Box 2226 Champaign, IL 61825*

QTY

The Fasting Cure by *Sinclair Upton* ISBN: *1-59462-222-1* **$13.95**
In the Cosmopolitan Magazine for May, 1910, and in the Contemporary Review (London) for April, 1910, I published an article dealing with my experiences in fasting. I have written a great many magazine articles, but never one which attracted so much attention... New Age/Self Help/Health Pages 164

Hebrew Astrology by *Sepharial* ISBN: *1-59462-308-2* **$13.45**
In these days of advanced thinking it is a matter of common observation that we have left many of the old landmarks behind and that we are now pressing forward to greater heights and to a wider horizon than that which represented the mind-content of our progenitors... Astrology Pages 144

Thought Vibration or The Law of Attraction in the Thought World ISBN: *1-59462-127-6* **$12.95**
by *William Walker Atkinson* Psychology/Religion Pages 144

Optimism by *Helen Keller* ISBN: *1-59462-108-X* **$15.95**
Helen Keller was blind, deaf, and mute since 19 months old, yet famously learned how to overcome these handicaps, communicate with the world, and spread her lectures promoting optimism. An inspiring read for everyone... Biographies/Inspirational Pages 84

Sara Crewe by *Frances Burnett* ISBN: *1-59462-360-0* **$9.45**
In the first place, Miss Minchin lived in London. Her home was a large, dull, tall one, in a large, dull square, where all the houses were alike, and all the sparrows were alike, and where all the door-knockers made the same heavy sound... Childrens/Classic Pages 88

The Autobiography of Benjamin Franklin by *Benjamin Franklin* ISBN: *1-59462-135-7* **$24.95**
The Autobiography of Benjamin Franklin has probably been more extensively read than any other American historical work, and no other book of its kind has had such ups and downs of fortune. Franklin lived for many years in England, where he was agent... Biographies/History Pages 332

Name	
Email	
Telephone	
Address	
City, State ZIP	

☐ Credit Card   ☐ Check / Money Order

Credit Card Number	
Expiration Date	
Signature	

Please Mail to: Book Jungle
PO Box 2226
Champaign, IL 61825
or Fax to: 630-214-0564

ORDERING INFORMATION

web: *www.bookjungle.com*
email: *sales@bookjungle.com*
fax: *630-214-0564*
mail: *Book Jungle PO Box 2226 Champaign, IL 61825*
or PayPal *to sales@bookjungle.com*

Please contact us for bulk discounts

DIRECT-ORDER TERMS

20% Discount if You Order Two or More Books
Free Domestic Shipping!
Accepted: Master Card, Visa, Discover, American Express

www.ingramcontent.com/pod-product-compliance
Lightning Source LLC
Chambersburg PA
CBHW080448170426
43196CB00016B/2725